Heaven on Earth!

*A Journey Through Modern Science
and the World Religions to the
Holy Eucharist*

R.A. Varghese

Maverick MultiMedia
New York

Testament Book House
228 Park Ave S #28214
New York, NY 10003

ISBN 978-1-087-94029-8

Copyright © 2023 by R.A. Varghese

All rights reserved. No part of this publication may be reproduced, stored in a retrieval system, or transmitted, in any form or by any means, electronic, mechanical, photocopying, recording, or otherwise, without the prior permission of Roy Abraham Varghese.

First published in 2013

Second edition 2018

Third edition 2022

R.A. Varghese is the author and/or editor of sixteen books on the interface of science, philosophy, and religion. His *Cosmos, Bios, Theos*, included contributions from 24 Nobel Prize-winning scientists. *Time* magazine called *Cosmos* "the year's most intriguing book about God." *Cosmic Beginnings and Human Ends*, a subsequent work, won a Templeton Book Prize for "*Outstanding Books in Science and Natural Theology*." His *The Wonder of the World* was endorsed by leading thinkers include two Nobelists and was the subject of an Associated Press story. He co-authored *There is a God—How the World's Most Notorious Atheist Changed His Mind* with Antony Flew (a book translated into Spanish, Portuguese, Korean, Russian, and Arabic). His most recent work, *The Missing Link* (2013), includes contributions from three Nobel Prize winners and scientists from Oxford, Cambridge, Harvard, and Yale. Varghese was a panelist at the science and religion forum in the Parliament of World Religions held in Chicago in 1993 and an invitee and participant in the Millennium World Peace Summit of Religious and Spiritual Leaders held at the United Nations in August 2000. Varghese has been interviewed on numerous radio and TV shows including *Coast to Coast*. He has also been profiled in different print publications.

For my three children
Michael Abraham Varghese
Mary Elizabeth Motwani
Rachel Esther Varghese

TABLE OF CONTENTS

The Divine Life Social Network 1

Chapter 1
To Understand the Eucharistic Invitation,
We Must Explore the Nature of the Divine
Life as Manifested to Humanity 7

LIFE
Chapter 2
The Eucharist Was Preserved from the
Beginning as a Mystical Secret That Brought
a New Race into Being 11

LIFE-TIME
Chapter 3
The Most Ancient and Universal World Religions
Prefigured Both the Doctrine and the Liturgy
of the Eucharist 15

LIFE-LINE
Chapter 4
The Chosen People Were Prepared for the Eucharist
with the Bread from Heaven, the Ritual of the Passover Sacrifice,
the Descent of the Divine Spirit, the Veneration of the Bread
of the Face of God and the Promise of a Pure Sacrifice to be
Celebrated Everywhere and at all times 21

LIFE-SAVER
Chapter 5

The Eucharist is Instituted by the Man Who Was God as a New and Eternal Covenant and a Partaking of the Life of God to be Celebrated Until the End of Time 29

- ❖ The narratives describing Jesus' institution of the Eucharist
- ❖ The problem of whether he meant what he said in the institution
- ❖ The question of whether the Eucharistic celebration was to be continued
- ❖ The issue of why we should believe Jesus' institution claim
- ❖ The redemptive sacrifice of Jesus and the forgiveness of sins
- ❖ Previews and postscripts of the Eucharist in the history of religions and their significance
- ❖ The roots of the Eucharist in the life of Israel
- ❖ The Eucharist as covenantal climax
- ❖ The Eucharist as a vehicle of the Divine Life
- ❖ The Eucharist as unparalleled parallel
- ❖ Christianity as THE Mystery Religion

LIFE-BOAT
Chapter 6

The New Testament, the First Christians and the Fathers of the Church Teach that the Eucharist is the Life Proclaimed by the Book of Life; that It Makes Us "Partakers of the Divine Nature" by Imparting to Us the Life of God; that It is a Participation in Jesus' Once-for-All Sacrifice on Calvary and His Perpetual Intercession before the Father; Testimonies to Its Divine Origin have continued throughout History; and It Draws us into the Eternal Self-Giving of the Holy Trinity.. 73

- ❖ How can we arrive at a credible and authoritative interpretation of the Eucharistic data?

- The logic of God (theos) – Theo-Logic – underlying the Eucharist
- The revelation of divinization, of the human transformed by receiving the Divine Life
- The roots of the Eucharist in Christian experience
- How the celebration of the Eucharist participates in the once- for-all event that was Calvary
- Celestial confirmation of the Eucharistic proclamation
- Participating in the Life of the Holy Trinity

LIFE-STORY
Chapter 7
The Eucharist is the Climax of the Book of Life that is the Universe as Apparent from the Progressive Elevation of Matter whereby the Hierarchy of Life in the Universe Ascends from Unicellular to Animal to Human Life Culminating in the Descent of the Divine Life 107

- How is divinization as it relates to the Eucharist different from other kinds of divinization?
- Why life provides a model in studying the Eucharist
- The hierarchy and progression of life
- The Author of the Book of life
- The Eucharist is creation out of something
- Transubstantiation
- How can bread and wine be transformed into Flesh and Blood?
- Transubstantiation in the light of the model of life
- Qualifications and caveats
- No dimensional presence in the Eucharist
- What does it mean to receive the Divine Life?

GOING-LIVE
Chapter 8
**The Eucharist is Eternal Life Here and Now,
the Life of Heaven**..137
- ❖ Beliefs of the Unbelievers
- ❖ Heaven as the Divine Biosphere
- ❖ The Eucharist and the Divine Force-Field
- ❖ The Eucharist as Energy-Source and Soul-Food
- ❖ The Blessed Virgin, Spouse of the Holy Spirit and Model of Divinization
- ❖ Sin, Holiness, Love and the Holy Mass

Appendix
**The Scientific Quest for the Origin of Life –
a Status Report from Researchers**...155

The Divine Life Social Network

The oldest and largest social network in the world is the Divine Life Social Life Network, namely the social network of those who receive the Life of God through the Holy Eucharist. "Eucharist" derives from the Greek "eucharistia" which means "thanksgiving." From the first century A.D., "Eucharist" referred to the liturgical celebration of the Lord's Supper, the sacred event at which food and drink were transformed into vehicles of the divine Life. "Eucharist" also refers to these vehicles themselves, the eucharistic elements that are proclaimed to be the Body and the Blood of God incarnate.

It is the contention of this book that the Eucharist makes sense of both the religious rituals of humanity and the very history of life in the Universe. It is the climax of both the history of religious worship and the history of the progressive elevation of matter. This is so because it is the transformational point in space and time when the physical becomes a vehicle of the Divine Life. The present work is a study of this great mystery, a mystery that was called for centuries the Discipline of the Secret and is today known as the Holy Sacrifice of the Mass and the Divine Liturgy.

In our study we will consider the Eucharistic story through the prism of a social networking site. All the familiar elements are "running on the site".

There is the Home Page and the User Profile where we explore the idea of the Life of God manifesting itself to humanity.

Then we have the Privacy Policy and the Terms and Conditions of the social network: this is where we go back in history to discover that the Eucharistic celebration was preserved for centuries as "The Secret": one had to consent to the Terms and Conditions of the social network before being admitted as a member.

What is a social network without "friends"? The Friends of the Divine Life Social Network are the world religions that preceded the incarnation of God in Jesus the Christ. They are "friends" because their beliefs and practices were eerie pre-figurations of the Eucharistic Event initiated by Jesus.

Apart from "friends", social networks also promote "groups", those friends who congregate around ideas and interests that are of special relevance to the network. Here we consider the people of Israel who embodied in their history and their identity the features that were to be amplified in the Eucharist: the Divine Word, the Temple of God, the sacrifice of thanksgiving, the descent of the Divine Spirit, the bread from Heaven, the promise of a pure offering that would be made from the rising of the sun to its setting in all nations.

Now we log in to the social network itself. And here we turn to an Event and a Post that lie at the center of the history of the Universe and the history of humanity. Here at the center we encounter the Savior of humanity, the Man who was God, the rendezvous of the religions. Jesus' Sacrifice on Calvary marked a re-start of history. Inextricably linked to this Event was a Post: his institution of the Eucharist, the transformation of bread and wine into a vehicle of his Divine Life, and his command that his followers partake of this sacrificial feast for all ages to come. For in partaking of his sacramentally present Body and Blood, they received his Life.

Which brings us to the share and care dimension of social networks, the Share, Follow Us and Like buttons. The institution of the Eucharist, the celebration of the Holy Mass, the distribution and reception of the vehicle of Divine Life are part of a bigger picture with its own "Theo-Logic" (*Theos*=God). This logic is laid out in the Hebrew Bible (the Old Testament) and the New Testament and articulated and proclaimed by the earliest Christian thinkers, the Fathers of the Church. Humans were created to receive the Life of God, to be divinized, to enter into the state of being that culminates in eternal union with their Creator. Divinization begins with baptism and culminates in the Eucharistic feast. The Divine Life Social Network exists precisely to "share" this Life. To "follow us" means to partake of the Life. And to partake of It is to "like" It, to be transformed at all levels. Moreover every celebration of the Eucharist is a participation in the once-for-all event of Calvary and the perpetual celestial intercession of the Son before the Father.

But there is more. The "writing on the wall" of the Divine Life Social Network is the history the Universe. There is a "Bio-logic" (*bios*=life) that parallels the Theo-logic. The Book of Life revealed to humanity (the Bible) and the Book of life unfolding in the history of the Universe arrive at the same destination, the Eucharist. The history of the Universe is a drama of the manifestation of progressively higher forms of life. It is a tale of the systematic elevation of matter that begins with the emergence of energy fields, then moves to unicellular life, plant and conscious life and finally arrives at rational self- conscious life. It reaches its climax with a transformation as dramatic as the initial emergence of energy: namely, the elevation of matter into a vehicle for the highest form of life, the Divine Life that underlies all of creation. Consequently, every instance of the genesis of life – from the cellular level to the creation of the conscious self – is a precursor of this utterly and unfathomably mysterious transmutation, the Gift of the Divine Life.

Finally, there is the "application" offered by the Divine Life Social Network. It is nothing less than entrance into Heaven here-and-now. For the end-"game" of this network is the Divine Biosphere, eternal ecstasy in union with the Creator of all things. As long as we live on earth, our participation in this divine dimension is sustained and deepened by incorporation into the sacral drama of the Mass and reception of the Bread from Heaven. When death arrives, it is, for those who live with the Life of God, the bursting into bloom of the seed planted in the soul by the Eucharistia.

This, then, is the exploration of the Divine Life Social Network that constitutes the present work.

From another perspective, we might also apply the metaphor of life in tracing the story of the Eucharist. Thus the chapter on the Discipline of the Secret falls under the sub-title of "life" because it concerns the first dissemination of the Divine Life. The next chapter considers the "life- time" of humanity because it studies the world religions as they existed from the dawn of history. This is followed by the "lifeline" thrown to humanity through the Chosen People. The rescue process comes to a climax with the "Life-Saver," Jesus, whose very name means he shall save his people from their sins. The Life given by him at the Last Supper and at Calvary is made available through the Eucharist which thus becomes humanity's "life-boat." From here we turn to the story of life in the Universe – "life-story" – which is a narrative of the appearance of new forms of life, each a quantum leap above its predecessor, until the grand finale when matter becomes a vehicle of the Divine Life. In the last chapter we go "live" as we discover what it means to live here and now with the Life of God.

The *claim* made by this book is that human beings have been invited to live with a new kind of life, the Life of God, to join what we call the Divine Life Social Network.

The *goal* of the book is to describe the means by which we can accept and take advantage of this astounding invitation.

The *architecture* of the book is sequential:

- first, we study the idea of what is meant by the Life of the God;
- second, we consider the initial explosive appearance of this invitation (called "the Secret") in all its glory on the horizon of human history;
- then we step backward to consider the original inklings of the invitation in ancient cultures, societies and religions culminating in the life-story of a nation that defined its identity in terms of the Divine;
- next we move to the full-blown issuance of the invitation by the very incarnation of the Divine Life;
- from here we follow up with a review of the two dimensions of the invitation, its Theo-logic and its Bio-logic: the Theo-logic concerns the change introduced in the human person who partakes of the Life of God ("divinization") and the Bio-logic concerns the

progressive elevation of matter in the Universe that begins with the emergence of unicellular life and reaches its climax in matter becoming a vehicle of the Divine Life ("Eucharist");
- finally we contemplate the end-point of receiving the Divine Life which is to enter into Life $\infty.0$, to live forever in the Divine Biosphere ("Heaven").

We will start our study now with the Home Page.

HOME PAGE OF THE DIVINE LIFE SOCIAL NETWORK

Chapter 1

To Understand the Eucharistic Invitation, We Must Explore the Nature of the Divine Life as Manifested to Humanity

The story of the Eucharist is the amazing announcement that the very Life of God is offered to us in a medium customized to our physicality and oriented to our transcendent destiny.

But what is meant by "the Life of God"? Here we turn to metaphors and analogies because we can only think and talk of God in analogies.

Consider biological life. The structure of a living organism is described by reference to its genome or genetic blueprint (the fixed set of genes present in all of its cells that control and transmit its characteristics). Here genome refers to the instruction sets that govern and constitute the life of an organism and that make an organism what it is.

Now Divine Life is a kind of life although it is not biological. The way in which God is alive lies beyond human comprehension because we are talking of the infinite-eternal Ground of Being whose Life has no limitation, no finitude, no beginning or end. But to advance our study, we will use the analogy of the Genome of God, the Life of God *as manifested to Homo sapiens*. To the extent that we as humans can partake of the Divine Life, to that extent it is possible for us to consider the vehicles and attributes of the Life of God manifested to, through and in the human reality. And much as investigators have "mapped" the genomes of humans and other species, here will try to map the Divine Genome. This is to say we will investigate *the instruction-sets that make the Divine Life present here and now*. We are studying the "genetic" switches, so to speak, that "turn on" the Life of God.

Our user community exists, then, to map the "Divine genome." We are the human race. The Divine Life Social Network is *our* response to the astounding claim that God has offered humanity the opportunity to subsist on the Divine Life, to partake of the elixir of eternity.

It is our contention here that the manifestation of the Divine Life is a phenomenon that unifies the history of the world religions and the narrative of modern science.

This is because the promise of the partaking of the Divine Life arises in the religious history of humanity and culminates with the Incarnation of God – *the humanizing of the Divine* – and the grant of the Divine Life through baptism and the Eucharist – *the divinizing of the human*.

With regard to the scientific study of the world, we note that the Divine Life is not terrestrial in origin or nature and therefore falls outside scientific study which is the analysis of the quantifiable. But since this Life is made available to terrestrial creatures it has implications for the physical. Hence we contemplate the scientific account of the origin and nature of different kinds of life in the Universe. And it is in this context that we come to see that the progressive elevation of matter in the history of the Universe reaches its climax and consummation in the descent of the Divine Life – a theophany most evident today in the Eucharistic celebration.

We were, in fact, configured for the Divine Life by the Alpha who is Omega. It is the transformational trajectory that fulfills human life by reinventing it.

The quest for the Divine Life, in fact, makes sense of human experience. The universal quest for meaning is complemented by the sense of an all-pervasive Presence that comes to us by drawing us. The vast majority of humanity has believed in a "wholly other" reality that interacts with the world of daily experience, a transcendent order of being that underlies all that we can see and touch. By transcendent we mean something that transcends, that is "above" all that is physical and material and has no limitations. But in parallel with this idea of the transcendent, many have had a sense of an immanent presence, a something that is "inside" but also lying beyond everything that is limited. In short, God as understood in human experience is both transcendent and immanent. Moreover there is the persistent idea that God will or has come "among us": God incarnate: one with humanity and yet fully Divine.

All of these thoughts and intuitions reach a climax in the recognition of the tri-personal God – the One God who is experienced as Transcendent, Immanent, Incarnate. It is in the light of this revelation that we begin to comprehend the "real world," the destiny to which all men and women are called – to be divinized, to share in the Divine nature, to participate in the Life of God. All of history centers on this Divine invitation and the endless present of eternity awaits those who accept it. This is the fundamental message not only of the world religions and the sages and the seers but of the Holy Bible.

"Out of the ground the LORD God made grow every tree that was delightful to look at and good for food, with *the tree of life* in the middle of the garden." *Genesis* 2:9

"Then the angel showed me the river of life-giving water … On either side of the river grew *the tree of life.*" *Revelation* 22:1-2

"Whoever eats my flesh and drinks my blood has eternal life." *John 6:54*

"We are the offspring of God." *Acts 17:39*

"I will pour out a portion of my spirit upon all flesh." *Joel 3:1, Acts 2:17*

"You will be able to share in the Divine nature." *2 Peter 1:4*

PRIVACY POLICY AND TERMS AND CONDITIONS
OF THE DIVINE LIFE SOCIAL NETWORK

Chapter 2

The Eucharist Was Preserved from the Beginning as a Mystical Secret That Brought a New Race into Being

From the first to the fifth centuries A.D., the Eucharistic celebration was a secret. In fact it was called the Discipline of the Secret. The Holy Mass was celebrated in hidden venues and described in code words. Attendance at the consecration was restricted to those who were trusted believers.

On one level, this secrecy was required because non-Christians would profane the ceremonies with ridicule. Then there were distorted descriptions of what was believed to take place giving rise to rumors of sorcery and cannibalism.

Fundamentally, however, the secrecy was driven by the recognition of the manifestation of the mystical. Central to the Secret was a remarkable vision: a new race had been called into being. The human had been reinvented, passing through the portal of Divine destiny.

The first, irrevocable step was to be cleansed at baptism, the fountain of re-creation. This was a process that began with the prospective disciple's recognition of the Incarnation of the infinite- eternal Absolute in space and time, of God taking on a human nature. Once this transcendent truth was accepted on the level of intellect and will, the prospect would be re-purposed and reprogrammed at the fountain of rebirth. And after the full assimilation of the revealed truths and a commitment to avoid evil, the probationer could become a participant in the sacral drama that was the Secret. This was the fearful and awesome moment when the things of earth were taken up into the heavens. This was the holy and glorious descent of the Divine order of being. This was the unthinkable climax of the history of terrestrial life when the Life of God entered the bloodstream of human being. For in receiving the elements consecrated at the Eucharistic celebration, the new believer partook of the Divine Life becoming a part of Discipline of the Secret, a member of the Divine Life Social Network.

The Discipline of the Secret meant that the leaders of the Christian movement were stewards of a treasure handed down from Heaven in the course of human history. They were entrusted and empowered with the mission of making the Divine Life present in the human milieu and of participating in an Act that affected the world and its history.

In the beginning was the Act. It was the humanizing of the Divine. It was the divinizing of the human. This is Its story.

From the beginning, the Fathers of the Church grasped the magnitude of what was taking place. "We become communicants in the Divine nature," wrote the intrepid Athanasius[1]. "We share the Divine, incomprehensible nature of God," said Cyril of Jerusalem.[2] "The action of this Divine energy," proclaimed Maximus the Confessor. "Bestows a more than ineffable pleasure and joy on him in whom the unutterable and unfathomable union with the Divine is accomplished. This, in the nature of things, cannot be perceived, conceived or expressed."[3]

The very majesty of what was taking place required the utmost discretion embodied by the Discipline of the Secret. In *Concerning those who are initiated into the Mysteries* (dating back to about 380 AD), Ambrose of Milan declaimed that "the mystery ought to remain sealed up with you, that it be not violated by the deeds of an evil life, and pollution of chastity, that it be not made known to thou, for whom it is not fitting." [4] Said Basil the Great, "the awful dignity of the mysteries is best preserved by silence." [5]

But if the Eucharistic Secret was indeed as transformational as its disciples proclaimed, how did its architecture relate to the history of humanity and of the universe? And what did it mean to say that we can partake of the Life of God or share in the Divine nature? And how can you join the Divine Life Social Network?

These are the urgent issues we will address as we move forward on our journey to the Life of God.

"FRIENDS" OF THE DIVINE LIFE
SOCIAL NETWORK

Chapter 3

The Most Ancient and Universal World Religions Prefigured Both the Doctrine and the Liturgy of the Eucharist

The promise of the Life of God embodied by the Eucharist was first recognized in the most ancient world religions. In this respect we might say that they served as a "beta test" of the Divine Life Social Network. We see them also as "friends" who prepared the human psyche for the acceptance and rapid dissemination of the Network when it was launched on the platform of world history. If God was going to bestow the unimaginable Gift of his Life it is wholly appropriate that he would prepare humanity for its coming.

The ancient religions pre-figured the Eucharist in their beliefs and their practices. They believed that the Divinely instituted sacred order of the Universe had been breached by human evil and that humanity had to perform sacrifice in expiation. "Sacrifice" means "make sacred" and it was believed that the Divine was present where sacrifice was performed. Fundamental to sacrifice was the idea of the blood covenant, blood being shed in atonement so as to bring about a restoration of union with the Divine. The blood of the sacrificial animal was identified with its life and this life was being offered up for the redemption of the offerors. The completion of the sacrifice required the offerors to partake of the flesh of the sacrificed animal so as to enter into communion with the Divine.

Sacrifice began at the very dawn of human history with the hunter-gatherers. The focus on atonement, covenant and communion was especially apparent in the elaborate ceremonies of the largest organized religions in the world of 1000 B.C., those of India, Persia, China, Israel and the Mediterranean societies.

In India we find the primordial prophecy of Prajapathi, the Supreme Spirit taking on human flesh and offering himself up for the redemption of humanity. Speaking of the Prajapathi sacrifice, Aravindaksha Menon writes that "in the Sathapadha Brahamana, a supplementary to the Yajurveda, seven attributes of the sacrifice of Prajapathi are explained.

1. At the time of sacrifice, the sacrificial victim would be crowned with a crown of thorns!
2. His hands and legs would be nailed to a wooden sacrificial post!
3. None of His bones be broken at that time!
4. Before death, He would be given a drink of "Somarasa" - the sour wine!
5. After death, His clothes would be divided among the afferors.
6. After death His body –flesh- would be eaten up by the offerors.
7. After death His blood would be drunk by the offerors."[1]

This prophesied sacrifice of Prajapathi underlies the sacrificial ceremonies prescribed in the holiest books of the Hindus, the Vedas. Krishnamohan Banerjea, a nineteenth century Indian thinker, observes that: "Numerous passages in the Sanhitas and Brahmanas of the Vedas drive us to the conclusion that sacrifices and oblations were considered the most sacred ceremonies in the primitive ritual of the Indo-Arians.

… As to the efficacy of sacrifices in human concerns, we find these prominent ideas in the Vedas, viz.—(1) The mystical identification of the sacrificer with the victim, which is the ransom for sin; (2) Sacrifice the great remedy for the ills of life—the ship or ark by which we escape sin and all worldly perils. (3) Sacrifice the instrument by which Sin and Death are annulled and abolished. … Sacrifice has accordingly been held in all Vedic treatises as the great remedy for sins and trespasses. It is at the same time both a satisfaction for heinous and moral offences, and an atonement for trivial mistakes and transgressions. Katyayana says that

Sacrifice procures heaven, and " heaven" is a word which stands for the highest happiness. The commentator of the *Taittiriya Sanhita* tells us that it is Nirriti or the Sin-deity that is a disturber of Sacrifices."[2]

Consumption of the flesh of the sacrificial victim is required for union with the Divine as pointed out in an article in *The Hindu*: "According to the Rigveda, the 'yagna pasu' (animal) should be a pure and spotless lamb. Thorns must be tightly tied around its head and the lamb must be tied to a pillar. The cloth covering the lamb must be shared by the people and not a bone of the lamb must be broken. To the fainting lamb, *Soma* [intoxicating juice from the soma plant] should be given. At the end of the sacrifice, there should be *prana prathista* to the lamb. The meat of this sanctified sacrificial lamb should be eaten."[3]

In Persia too there is a prophesy of a final Savior who will judge the world and bring about the resurrection of the dead. Sacrifice is central to the Avesta, the holy book of the Persians. The haoma plant, which represents God become man, is offered as a sacrifice and the juice which results from the ritual confers immortality on those who partake of it. According to Geoffrey Parrinder, "In this bloodless sacrifice the offering is at once god, priest and victim, and the faithful consume the Divine sacrifice in anticipation of the sacrifice at the end of the world which will make all humans immortal."[4]

Says J. Lindsay, "the Haoma plant ... was identified with the Son of God who was bruised and mangled in the mortar so that the life-giving fluid from his body might give new strength to his worshippers."[5] According to another Persian scholar, "Haoma is accompanied by righteousness and piety. (10:8, Yt 17:5) It confers immortality. It is the source of righteousness. (10:4)."[6]

In China, for some four thousand years it was believed that sacrifice to God (understood monotheistically) was required to maintain the cosmic order, what the Chinese called the Mandate of Heaven. The most important sacrifice was the Border Sacrifice which had to be performed annually by the Emperor himself in a solemn series of ceremonies that mirrored the Levitical rituals of the ancient Jews (for instance, the sacrificial victim had to be an unblemished first-born animal). The sacrificial ceremony is only complete with communion. In *Faith of Our Fathers – God in Ancient China*, Chan Kei Thong points out that "At the emperor's annual sacrifice at the Altar of Heaven, the altar for sacrifice and the tables for meals are placed in close proximity. In fact, so prominent a feature was the feasting at the yearly sacrifices that one foreign scholar said, "The Chinese idea of a sacrifice to the supreme ruler of Heaven and Earth is that of a banquet. Access to God is obtained by the shedding of blood (at the altar), after which the emperor can enjoy communion with God at the meal (the table)."[7]

Sacrifice was tied to the Chinese idea of a covenant with Heaven just as in Israel. In fact, "the Chinese word translated as "covenant" is (xue meng), which literally means "blood covenant." Thong points out that "Both the Hebrew and Chinese historical records reveal a belief in the necessity of the death of a perfect sacrifice to cover the sins of the nation."[8]

As for the Mediterranean societies, the noted authority on antiquity Walter Burkert points out that, "Animal sacrifice was an all-pervasive reality in the ancient world. The Greeks did not perceive much difference between the substance of their customs, and those of the Egyptians and Phoenicians, Babylonians and Persians, Etruscans and Romans, though ritual details varied greatly among the Greeks themselves. …. And yet whatever complexities, layers, and changes in cultural tradition underlie the individual peculiarities, it is astounding, details aside, to observe the similarity of action and experience from Athens to Jerusalem and on to Babylon."[9]

Especially striking in the sacrifices across the ancient world was the idea of the blood covenant. In his classic work, *The Blood Covenant*, Henry Clay Trumbull pointed out that "the transference of blood from one organism to another has been counted the transference of life, with all that life includes. The inter-commingling of blood by its inter-transference has been understood as equivalent to an inter- commingling of natures. Two natures inter-commingled, by the inter- commingling of blood, have been considered as forming, thenceforward, one blood, one life, one nature, one soul – in two organisms. The inter-commingling of natures by the inter- commingling of blood has been deemed possible between man and a lower organism, – even between man and Deity, actually or by symbol."[10]

It should be said here that there are sacrifices and there are sacrifices. In some ancient peoples, the initial impetus of atonement, purification and union with the Divine (seen as the Supreme Spirit) devolved into savagery and horrendous evil. Sacrifice for the most part involved animals or grain and wine. In certain societies, however, the practice degenerated into the darkness of human sacrifice. Bizarre and gory offerings to bloodthirsty gods and goddesses, occultic superstitions, anthropomorphic ideas of the Divine, polytheism and idolatry proliferated over time. Nevertheless in the teachings and practices of the most ancient organized religions – in India, China, Persia and Israel – there is a commonality of theme that is astonishing. Distortions there were but underneath it all there is a constant focus on turning to the Most High and a sense of urgency about maintaining the cosmic order through sacrifice followed by communion.

This review of the ancient world religions indicates that virtually all peoples at all times – individually and institutionally – sought to participate in the Life of God. It seems obvious too that Divine Providence was preparing the human race to comprehend, appreciate and receive the greatest of gifts.

"GROUPS" IN THE DIVINE LIFE SOCIAL NETWORK

Chapter 4

The Chosen People Were Prepared for the Eucharist with the Bread from Heaven, the Ritual of the Passover Sacrifice, the Descent of the Divine Spirit, the Veneration of the Bread of the Face of God and the Promise of a Pure Sacrifice to be Celebrated Everywhere and at all times

Among the ancient nations of the world, the relevance of the people of Israel for the revelation of the Eucharist is especially striking. One could say that they prophetically embodied in their history, identity and life, the promise of the Eucharist. We can even speak of them as the Group that blossomed into the Divine Life Social Network.

The Eucharistic dimension of the Jewish experience is easily apparent: the obligation of performing sacrifices, especially the Passover sacrifice where the lamb takes on the sin of the people of Israel, and the need to partake of the flesh of the sacrificial animal; the link between sacrifice and the Hebraic covenant with God; the prophecy of the coming of the Messiah of Israel and of the Suffering Servant who would take on himself the punishment for the sins of the people; the Manna from Heaven miraculously provided in the desert that would be bestowed again in the Messianic Age; the affirmation that the Todah sacrifice of thanksgiving would never cease and that a pure offering would be offered in all lands from the rising of the sun to its setting; the veneration of the Bread of the Face of God; and the astounding phenomenon of the Spirit of God "filling" those who were united with the will of God.

A short description of each of these features indicates their relevance.

The history of Israel is, above all, a history of their direct interaction with the Divine. Underlying this interaction was a partnership or covenant between God and the people of Israel. The covenant came into being because of the obedience of Abraham, the father of the Israelites, and was later amplified under Moses, their greatest leader. In both cases, the covenant was ratified with sacrifice. The exodus of the Israelites from Egypt under Moses was commemorated (under Divine command) by the annual Passover sacrifice in which an unblemished lamb was sacrificed and its flesh consumed by the priests and the people.

Mosaic law called for a superstructure of sacrifices. Among the most important sacrifices was the peace offering called the Todah sacrifice. "Todah" means "thank offering" (*eucharistia* in Greek); it was offered in thanksgiving for deliverance from grave danger including death. Martin Barrack notes that "The ancient rabbis believed that when the Messiah would come all sacrifices except the Todah would cease, but the Todah would continue for all eternity. In 70 AD the Temple fell to earth and all of the bloody animal sacrifices stopped. Only the Todah remains, the eucharistia, the Final Sacrifice at which the last words spoken are Todah l'Adonai, 'Thanks be to God.'"[1]

The prophecy of the coming of a Messiah who would usher in a new era and whose kingdom is everlasting is a central element of Judaism. Three other related biblical prophecies are similarly significant: the promise of a new covenant with God that will be written on the human heart, the narrative of a suffering servant who would redeem his people from their sins by his death and the vision of a pure "grain offering" that would be offered in every nation "from the rising of the sun even to its setting."

Aligned with the Messianic prophecy was the belief that the miraculous manna that rained down from Heaven to the Israelites in the desert would be given again in the age of the Messiah. Brant Pitre points out:

Since the rabbis believed that the manna continued to exist in heaven, even after it had ceased on earth, many of them were waiting for the manna to return one day. And since they also believed that the Messiah would be a new Moses, many of them expected that the return of the manna would take place at the coming of the Messiah.....

According to the Midrash Rabbah, "As the first redeemer caused manna to descend, as it is stated, 'Because I shall cause to rain bread from heaven for you' (Exodus 16:4), so will the latter redeemer cause manna to descend" (Ecclesiastes Rabbah 1:9). In other words, just as the first Moses gave Israel manna from heaven, so too would the new Moses – the Messiah – bring down bread from heaven.[2]

Also vital was the so-called showbread reserved in the Temple (Lev 7:20). Pitre has shown that it is more accurate to call it the Bread of the Face of God:

Some scholars argue that the expression [for *lehem ha panim*, the Hebrew phrase earlier translated as showbread] should be translated as literally as possible. They point out that the word commonly rendered as *presence* is actually the Hebrew word for *face (panim)*. Therefore, the most literal translation of the Hebrew is *the Bread of the Face*. From this perspective the meaning of the expression is clear, but the implications are enormous: the Bread of the Presence is nothing less than the Bread of the Face *of God*. In this view, somehow, the bread itself is a visible sign of the face of God.[3]

The role of the Bread of the Face has been rarely realized. In his superb study, Pitre lays out its monumental significance:

When we look at the pages of the Old Testament, it should be quite clear that the Bread of the Presence stood at the very center of Israelite worship. Alongside the famous Ark of the Covenant and the golden Menorah, it was one of the three most sacred objects in the Holy Place, the inner sanctum of the ancient Tabernacle.

No one doubts how important the Sabbath was in ancient Israel; the Bread of the Presence was *the* Sabbath sacrifice, the "most holy" offering. Finally, it was both the sign of the "everlasting covenant" with Israel and the Bread of the Lord's perpetual presence in the Tabernacle – the "bread of the Face" of Almighty God. Clearly, according to Jewish Scripture, the mysterious Bread of the Presence was no ordinary bread. ...

Moreover, we learn that certain rabbis believed that something special happened to the Bread of the Presence when it was offered by the priests as a sacrifice to God. *Before* the bread was brought into the Holy Place to be offered in sacrifice, it could be laid on a marble table. But *after* the bread had been consecrated to God by the priests, it had to be laid on a golden table: In the Porch at the entering in of the House [=the Temple] were two tables, the one of marble and the other of gold. *On the table of marble they laid the Bread of the Presence when it was brought in and on the table of gold they laid the Bread of the Presence when it was brought out*, since what is holy must be raised [in honor] and not brought down. And within was a table of gold whereon the Bread of the Presence lay continually. (Mishnah, Menahoth 11:7). ...

One other tradition even goes so far as to suggest that the Bread of the Presence, after it had been consecrated, actually displayed *supernatural properties*. After the priests took the bread out of the Holy Place, they would lay it on the "table of gold, "so that they might eat it among themselves (Mishnah, Menahoth 11:7). ...

According to both the Jerusalem Talmud and Babylonian Talmud, at each of [Israel's three annual] feasts, the priests in the Temple would do something remarkable. They would remove the Golden Tables of the Bread of the Presence from within the Holy Place so that the Jewish pilgrims could see it. When they removed the holy bread, the priests would elevate it and say the following words: "They [the priests] used to lift it [the Golden Table] up and exhibit the Bread of the Presence on it to those who came up for the festivals, saying to them, '"Behold, God's love for you!'" (Babylonian Talmud, Menahoth 29A)

"Three times a year shall all your males see *the face of the Lord*, the LORD God of Israel" (Exodus 34:23; 23:17). In this line, the Hebrew word for the "face" of God is *panim*, the same word used for the "Bread of the Presence" or "Bread of the Face" (Exodus 25:30). In other words, by showing the pilgrims the Bread of the *panim*, the priests in the Temple were fulfilling the Law that commanded that they "see the Face" of the Lord. As the Jewish scholar Israel Knohl writes: "It seems to me that the sages departed from convention and permitted the display of the Temple furniture before the pilgrims so as to allow them to fulfill their obligation 'to see the face.' Or, to put it another way, the presentation of these holy items before the large assembly created the experience of a public theophany. The Israelites who had longed for the Temple courts and asked 'when may I come to see the face of God,' went up to the Temple at the pilgrimage feast and gazed upon the vessels of the Temple-service that were brought out of hiding. In this way their spiritual thirst was slaked and they fulfilled the commandment of the Torah that 'three times a year each male must see the face of the Sovereign, the LORD, the God Israel.'" (Exodus 34:23). … It seems reasonable to conclude that for ancient Jews, the Bread of the Presence was not the *actual* face of God but an earthly sign of his face. …

According to ancient Jewish tradition, this holy bread was the primordial sacrifice of Melchizedek, the miraculous food of the Holy Place, the Bread of the Face of Almighty God. Last but not least, this holy bread was a living, visible sign of God's love for his people, the way his earthly people could catch a fleeting glimpse of the ultimate desire of their hearts: to see the face of God and live, and to know that he loved them.[4]

Finally, the Hebrew Bible gives us the first glimmer of the phenomenon that later came to be called "divinization," the phenomenon whereby human beings come to share the Divine Life.

The drama of divinization began at creation when "God created man in his image; in the Divine image he created him." (Genesis 1:27). Yet this grand human experiment almost died at birth. Defy the Divine will and "you will be like gods," (Genesis 3:5) promised the Deceiver. But he dealt in counterfeits and half-truths. *Humans were built to be God-like – but there could be no divinizing without God.* Such a cutting of the cord was, in fact, dehumanizing. Its fruits were instant death and destruction.

Despite this catastrophe, the Divine blueprint for humankind remained what it was from the start – a plan to endow homo sapiens with the Divine Life. Previewing this destiny were the prophets and patriarchs, priests and kings, judges and warriors of God who were "filled" with his Spirit.

Consider a few notable examples of divinization from the Hebrew Bible.

Joseph: Joseph was "a man so endowed with the spirit of God." (Genesis 41:38).

Moses: Moses was not only filled with the Spirit but the Lord bestowed his Spirit on those who helped him in his mission. "The Lord then came down in the cloud and spoke to him. Taking some of the spirit that was on Moses, he bestowed it on the seventy elders; and as the spirit came to rest on them, they prophesied." Said Moses at one point: 'Would that all the people of the Lord were prophets! Would that the Lord might bestow his spirit on them all!'" (Numbers 11:25,29).

Joshua: And the Lord replied to Moses: 'Take Joshua, son of Nun, a man of spirit, and lay your hand upon him.'" (Numbers 27:18).

Othniel: "The spirit of the Lord came upon him, and he judged Israel." (Judges 3:10).

Gideon: "The spirit of the Lord enveloped Gideon." (Judges 6:34).

Jephthah: "The spirit of the Lord came upon Jephthah." (Numbers 11:29).

Samson: "The spirit of the Lord came upon Samson and he tore the lion to pieces as one tears a lamb." (Numbers 14:6).

David: "Then Samuel, with the horn of oil in hand, anointed him in the midst of his brothers; and from that day on, the spirit of the Lord rushed upon David." (1 Samuel 16:13).

The prophets of the Chosen People revealed the coming of an age when all peoples on earth would receive the outpouring of the Divine Spirit:

"I will pour my spirit upon all mankind. Your sons and daughters shall prophesy, your old men shall dream dreams, your young men shall see visions; Even upon the servants and the handmaids, in those days, I will pour out my spirit. And I will work wonders in the heavens and on the earth." (Joel 3:1-3).

"I will give you a new heart and place a new spirit within you, taking from your bodies your stony hearts and giving you natural hearts. I will put my spirit within you and make you live by my statutes, careful to observe my decrees." (Ezekiel 36:27-8).

"Hear then, O Jacob, my servant, Israel, whom I have chosen, … I will pour out my spirit upon your offspring, and my blessing upon your descendants." (Is 44:1,3).

It is the underlying engine of divinization that energized the nation's three powerhouses: Torah, Todah and Temple. The Torah bestowed Divine truth. The Todah and the other sacrifices removed barriers to Divine union. And the Temple was the earthly seat of the Divine Presence, the Shekinah. All three also pointed to a mysterious leader of the future and a singular event that offered humanity the opportunity to subsist on the Divine Life, to partake of the elixir of eternity.

THE EVENT, *THE* POST THAT BROUGHT INTO BEING THE DIVINE LIFE SOCIAL NETWORK

Chapter 5

The Eucharist is Instituted by the Man Who Was God as a New and Eternal Covenant and a Partaking of the Life of God to be Celebrated Until the End of Time

"Out of the ground the LORD God made grow every tree that was delightful to look at and good for food, with the tree of life in the middle of the garden." Genesis 2:9

"Then the angel showed me the river of life-giving water … On either side of the river grew the tree of life." Revelation 22:1-2

"Keep secret the message and seal the book until the end time." Daniel 12:4

"The mystery hidden from ages and from generations past. But now it has been manifested to his holy ones." Colossians 1:36

Whereas events and posts are normally activities within a social network, it was an Event and a Post that created the Divine Life Social Life Network. The "Event" was the incarnation of the Son of God, Jesus the Anointed One, and his redemptive sacrifice of himself on Calvary. The "Post" was his institution of the Holy Eucharist as the vehicle of his Life to be offered up and partaken of until the end of time.

The Eucharistic proclamation must be considered at several levels:

- ❖ The narratives describing Jesus' institution of the Eucharist
- ❖ The problem of whether he meant what he said in the institution
- ❖ The question of whether the Eucharistic celebration was to be continued
- ❖ The issue of why we should believe Jesus' institution claim
- ❖ The redemptive sacrifice of Jesus and the forgiveness of sins
- ❖ Previews and postscripts of the Eucharist in the history of religions and their significance
- ❖ The roots of the Eucharist in the life of Israel
- ❖ The Eucharist as covenantal climax
- ❖ The Eucharist as a vehicle of the Divine Life
- ❖ The Eucharist as unparalleled parallel
- ❖ Christianity as THE Mystery Religion

Each one of these facets should be considered to grasp the gravity and magnitude of the proclamation. The foundation, of course, is Jesus' institution of the Eucharist. The centrality of the institution is highlighted by its pivotal positioning in all four Gospels, in the Acts of the Apostles and in St. Paul.

Jesus' institution of the Eucharist

The denouement of the drama of divinization is a startling and utterly unique proclamation

> "The Jewish feast of Passover was near. … Jesus answered and said to them, … 'I am the bread of life. Your ancestors ate the manna in the desert, but they died; this is the bread that comes down from heaven so that one may eat it and not die. I am the living bread that came down from heaven; whoever eats this bread will live forever; and the bread that I will give is my flesh for the life of the world.' The Jews quarreled among themselves, saying: 'How can this man give us [his] flesh to eat?' Jesus said to them, 'Amen, amen, I say to you, unless you eat the flesh of the Son of Man and drink his blood, you do not have life within you. Whoever eats my flesh and drinks my blood has eternal life, and I will raise him on

the last day. For my flesh is true food, and my blood is true drink. Whoever eats my flesh and drinks my blood remains in me and I in him. Just as the living Father sent me and I have life of the Father, so also the one who feeds on me will have life because of me. This is the bread that came down from heaven. Unlike your ancestors who ate and still died, whoever eats this bread will live forever.'" (John 6:4,43,48-58).

Jesus' proclamation in the Gospel of John is amplified and unified in a triptych of complementary pronouncements in the Synoptic Gospels:

"The disciples then went off, entered the city, and found it just as he had told them; and they prepared the Passover. ... While they were eating, he took bread, said the blessing, broke it, and gave it to them, and said, "Take it; this is my body." Jesus "took bread, said the blessing, broke it, and gave it to them, and said, 'Take it, this is my body.' Then he took a cup, gave thanks, and gave it to them, and they all drank from it. He said to them, 'This is my blood of the covenant, which will be shed for many.'" (Mark 14:12, 22-4).

"The disciples then did as Jesus had ordered, and prepared the Passover. ... While they were eating, Jesus took the bread, said the blessing, broke it, and giving it to his disciples said, 'Take and eat; this is my body.' Then he took a cup, gave thanks, and gave it to them, saying, 'Drink from it, all of you, for this is my blood of the covenant, which will be shed on behalf of many for the forgiveness of sins.'" (Matthew 26:17,26-28).

"He said to them, 'I have eagerly desired to eat this Passover with you before I suffer, for I tell you, I shall not eat it [again] until there is fulfillment in the kingdom of God.' Then he took a cup, gave thanks and said, 'Take this and share it among yourselves; for I tell you [that] from this time on I shall not drink of the fruit of the vine until the kingdom of God comes.' Then he took the bread, said the blessing, broke it, and gave it to them, saying, 'This is my body, which will be given for you; do this in memory of me.' And likewise the cup after they had eaten, saying, 'This cup is the new covenant in my blood, which will be shed for you.'" (Luke 22:15-20).

Taken as they stand in all their prima facie force, these utterances are bewildering and yet believable precisely because they are so unbelievable. Certainly those who heard them took them seriously either by taking them at their face value and centering their lives on these "words of eternal life" or by rejecting them in toto and returning "to their former way of life." At one level, the denouement made no sense. At another level, it made sense of everything – of all of religious history and of human existence. It was an unparalleled parallel. The world religions had peered at the phenomenon through a telescope. Now here it was in all its glory – no mists of time to obscure it, no problems of perspective to cloud it.

A new kind of life had been unleashed on that night of institution, a Divine Life that swept across the world by entering the souls and hearts of all who said Yes. For there was no mistaking what was being said: "Whoever eats my flesh and drinks my blood has eternal life." This was the sacred mystery. This was the Secret.

The basic message was clear: humanity is called to live with the Life of God: the human person will now by powered by Divine energy. It was an astonishing teaching – but one which was preached and practiced from the very beginning of the new dispensation.

"I live, no longer I, but Christ lives in me," proclaimed the Apostle Paul (Galatians 2:20). "For the Son of God became man so that we might become God," said Athanasius. [1] "He gave us divinity, we gave him humanity," said Ephraem of Syria.[2] "He gives a sharing in the Divine life by making himself food for those whom he knows and who have received from him the same sensibility and intelligence," wrote Maximus. "Thus in tasting the food they know with a true knowledge the Lord is good, he who mixes in a Divine quality to deify those who eat, since he is and is clearly called bread of life and of strength."[3]

The ancient Coptic liturgy of St. Mark, like all the other ancient liturgies, was instituted to make this mysterious command a living reality: "And this bread he makes into his Holy Body, Our Lord God and Saviour Jesus

Christ, given for the remission of sins and eternal life to those who shall partake of him. And this cup also, into the precious Blood of his new covenant."

The ancient Councils of the Church took the descent of the Divine Life for granted: "Proclaiming the death, according to the flesh, of the Only-begotten Son of God, that is Jesus Christ, confessing his resurrection from the dead, and his ascension into heaven, we offer the Unbloody Sacrifice in the churches, and so go on to the mystical thanksgivings, and are sanctified, having received his Holy Flesh and the Precious Blood of Christ the Saviour of us all. And not as common flesh do we receive it; God forbid: nor as of a man sanctified and associated with the Word according to the unity of worth, or as having a Divine indwelling, *but as truly the Life-giving and very flesh of the Word himself.* For he is the Life according to his nature as God, and when he became united to his Flesh, he made it also to be Life- giving."[4]

The problem of whether he meant what he said in the institution

Given the astounding nature of Jesus' proclamation, professed Christians in later centuries have tried to "tame" it to conform to what they think is reasonable. Jesus was being symbolic not literal, they say. But this revisionist approach faces a huge obstacle. First, there are the texts themselves that do not show any sign of being "symbolic." Then there is the interpretation of these texts by the first Christians and the Christian community as a whole for over a thousand years who took Jesus at his word. Literally.

The earliest Christians lived and taught the truth that he literally meant what he said when he revealed that bread and wine would become his body and blood. St. Ignatius of Antioch, on his way to martyrdom in Rome in 107 A.D., even said that a denial of this truth went contrary to the mind of God: "Take note of those who hold heterodox opinions on the grace of Jesus Christ which has come to us, and see how contrary their opinions are to the mind of God ... They abstain from the Eucharist and from prayer because they do not confess that the Eucharist is the flesh of our Savior Jesus Christ, flesh which suffered for our sins and which that Father, in his goodness, raised up again. They who deny the gift of God are perishing in their disputes."[5]

Textually too, the relevant words can hardly admit of divergent interpretations. The Gospels and St. Paul testify unanimously to the "institution." Although the discourses in the Gospel of John are rich in symbolism, Jesus pointedly distinguishes between the symbolic and the literal. "The language of John 6," writes Robert Sungenis. "Contains a dramatic shift from merely figurative wording to intensely literal wording, as even the Jews themselves forthrightly notice (verse 52)."[6] Jesus was willing to suffer the loss of many who followed him and even risk the loss of all his closest followers. If he was simply being symbolic, he could have made an announcement to this effect thus averting the resultant scandal. Rudolf Bultmann, the New Testament theologian best-known for his rejection of traditional doctrine, admits that John 6:54-58 has to be taken literally: "It is a matter of real eating and not simply of some sort of spiritual participation."[7] Instead of using the generic Greek term for eating, John 6:51ff. uses a word that cannot be viewed symbolically since it refers to masticating one's food.[8] The philosopher Elizabeth Anscombe points out that "eating flesh" and "drinking blood" are unlikely candidates for symbolism: "For why would anyone want to eat someone's flesh or drink his blood? 'I will drink your blood' might be a vow made against an enemy. Indeed in Old Testament language eating a man's flesh and drinking his blood is an idea expressive of just such deadly enmity."[9]

Certainly all Jews would have been shocked by Jesus' commandment to drink his blood in view of Old Testament prohibitions against drinking blood. But Joachim Jeremias points out that this very fact should show that the institution could only have come from the progenitor of the new movement. "Exactly that which seems scandalous will be historical."[10] More recently Otto Betz makes this same point: Since the Jews were forbidden to drink blood, this command has to be attributed to Jesus and not the early Church.[11]

The philosopher and historian of science Stanley Jaki points out the institution narratives in the first three Gospels are intended to be taken literally:

> As long as one is ready to read the account of the Last Supper in its plain words, it is not possible to escape the conclusion that Christ held his own body and blood in his hands when he said

'This is my body which is given up for you,' and 'This cup is the cup of the new covenant in my blood.' The verb *is* in the English follows the Greek *esti* in the Gospel of Mark and Luke, both written in Greek, and the Greek of Matthew's Gospel, originally composed in Hebrew, which uses no such a verb in demonstrative phrases. The text allows no room for a figurative sense. One may speculate how a bread can also be a human body, but only after one has taken the multiplication of the bread for a true miracle. That multiplication touched off such wonder in some who witnessed it at close range that they recorded it with an accuracy that should astound the perceptive reader of the Gospels, especially in these modern times when scientific accuracy is held so high. … [Through his miracles Jesus] proved that he had a supreme power over things physical, including his own physical body. He stilled the stormy lake by a single word. He walked on the waves as if he could defy that most universally binding physical force which is the force of gravity. He made the dead come alive."[12]

St. Paul, one of the earliest leaders of the Christian Church, dramatically echoes the literal view: "Anyone who eats and drinks without discerning the body, eats and drinks judgment on himself. That is why many among you are ill and infirm, and a considerable number are dying." (I Corinthians 11:30). This passage indicates that "the breaking of the bread", which had become a fundamental part of the movement (Acts 2:42), was not simply an exercise in symbolism. It had observable effects and unworthy participation was an invitation to sickness, even to death. And this was a teaching that St. Paul "received from the Lord" – the very same Lord who taught that those who wished to receive eternal life should eat his flesh and drink his blood!

About this passage, Jaki writes, "The warning [of 1 Cor 11:26-27] made no sense unless the bread and wine were really the body and blood of Christ. Only then did it make sense for Paul to insist that to partake in the body and blood while having sins on one's conscience was to eat and drink a fearsome judgment against oneself."[13]

The question of whether the Eucharistic celebration was to be continued

But did Jesus intend the Eucharistic celebration to continue after the Last Supper? Or was it a one-time event?

The institution narrative reported by Luke includes a mandate: "Do this in memory of me." It is a command to perform something "in memory". What is this something? The "this" refers to the offering of the Jesus' body, an act which by its very nature as an offering up is a sacrifice.

It is clear, of course, that the "this" in "Do this in memory of me" does not refer to the nature of the eucharistic elements. Rather, it is obvious from the text that it refers to a ritual, in this case a sacrificial ritual.

The word used for "in memory" is *anamnesis*, one out of nine other possible words in Greek with the same meaning. This particular word is used precisely because it is exclusively associated with sacrifice. As used here, writes Sungenis, "*anamnesis* does not refer merely to remembering a past event or a past sacrifice; rather it refers to remembrance brought about by the act of sacrifice."[14] Eric Mascall, Anglican philosopher and theologian, adds: "*Anamnesis* means not a psychological act of remembering but a genuine recalling into the present of an act which is past as an event of history but is eternalised in the heavenly places. … it is … a sacramental instantiation, of the tremendous act and event itself."[15] In short, *the mandate is a call for a commemorative sacrifice not for the commemoration of a sacrifice.*

Again, as reported by Matthew, Mark and Luke, the words of institution are linked to a covenant, namely a new covenant between God and humanity. Significantly, the only time that Jesus uses the word "covenant" is on this momentous occasion. The covenants of Israel were sealed with the blood of the sacrificial victim. Here the speaker not only announces a New Covenant but specifies that the Blood that would seal it was to be his own (and this Blood is miraculously provided, an idea nowhere found in the Hebrew Bible). "The biblical accounts," writes Brant Pitre, "strongly suggest that Jesus is replacing the 'flesh' of the Passover lamb (Exodus 12:8) with his own body and the 'blood' of the Passover lamb (Exod. 12:13, 22-27) with his own blood. Hence, by means of this final enacted sign, Jesus is *prophetically reconstituting the Passover sacrifice around his own suffering and death*, with himself as the new Passover lamb."[16]

He commands his followers to continue the covenantal offering of his Body and Blood ("do this") because it is through this offering that the new covenant is renewed and re-presented. And whereas the Paschal Meal of the Old Covenant was consumed in memory of Yahweh, the New Paschal Meal is centered on the Testator of the New Covenant ("Do this in remembrance of me.").

In fact it is this Paschal Meal that reveals the true mission of the man who called himself "the Son of Man": his Blood is offered up "on behalf of many for the forgiveness of sins." Moreover, as Pitre emphasizes, "*by means of the Last Supper, Jesus transformed the Cross into a Passover, and by means of the Cross, he transformed the Last Supper into a sacrifice.*"[17]

The issue of why we should believe Jesus' institution claim – the question of who he is

Now a message is only as credible as its source. This is especially the case when we go beyond familiar and tangible settings. The existence of three dimensional beings (with length, breadth and height) cannot be proved or disproved within a world of two dimensions (of length and breadth). Likewise the truth of a teaching that goes beyond the "natural" cannot be proved or disproved using laws of nature. The truth of such an extra-natural teaching depends entirely on the authority of its originator. And when we talk of the Divine Life, the ultimate guarantor of veracity would have to be the Divine itself.

Thus the proclamation of the gift of Divine Life can only be accepted if the proclaimer was Divine. And yet we know, from the records themselves, that the one who proclaimed this gift was a man, Jesus of Nazareth. So why should he be taken at his word?

This question has been explored in some detail in the books *The Christ Connection – How the World Religions Prepared the Way for the Phenomenon of Jesus* and *How We Know that Jesus is God and Man – the Incarnation of Infinity*. But a brief overview will be helpful.

To say Jesus of Nazareth is God incarnate is to affirm that God manifested his Triune (Three-in-One) Being and Action in the existence of Jesus of Nazareth. Jesus was the locus of the divine in human terms. From start to finish, from conception, baptism and ministry to death, resurrection and ascension, Jesus' life was above all a manifestation of the tri-personal God: he was the Son, filled with the Holy Spirit, doing the Will of his Father. Every human person is made in the image of God. Jesus is a divine Person in the image of man: The Triune SIM card/network/power-source in the human smartphone.

Consider the cumulative case for the affirmation that Jesus is God incarnate:

1	Claim to be God Incarnate
	First and foremost, Jesus claimed to be God incarnate and his followers understood him to make this claim. This is why he was crucified, his followers persecuted. Jesus' divine claim was made in the terms understood by the Jews of his time: e.g., claiming to have the attributes proper to God such as forgiving sins; taking the divine Name ("I AM"); placing himself on the same level as the Torah, the Word of God, and the Temple, the dwelling-place of God. He was acclaimed as God united to a human nature by his followers right from the first century as is evident from their writings. Jesus is the only "founder" of a world religion to make this claim about himself. Minimally, only such a claim would make it worth our while to study a claim of divine revelation. This is because only God incarnate could authoritatively tell us the truth about God and ourselves. A prophet or sage who is solely and simply human can only speak as one who believes and not as one who knows. Only God incarnate can KNOW. Hence only the revelation of God incarnate has the seal of divine truth.

2   Resurrection from the Dead

Jesus was the only person of whom it is claimed: he rose from the dead and continues to be active in human life and history. The testimony of the transformed apostles and the entire church from its earliest days to the present is singular in its unanimity and consistency: the crucified Jesus physically rose from the dead. The most compelling feature of the claim of resurrection is the transformation of the followers of Jesus and the genesis of the Christian movement. What transformed eleven fearful peasants and fisher-folk into superheroes who preached the Good News across the world despite trials and tribulations and eventually horrendous deaths? What galvanized them to take on the most powerful empire of the day? The hallucination hypothesis is not remotely plausible for those who know the causes and characteristics of hallucinations (an individual experience, drugs, mental illness, an expectation of seeing that which is allegedly witnessed – none of which apply in the present case). The idea of a hoax is wildly implausible given the improbability that anyone would embrace a gruesome end in order to perpetrate a fiction. These kinds of counter- explanations remind us of what George Orwell once said, "One has to belong to the intelligentsia to believe things like that. No ordinary man could be such a fool." The Jewish rabbi Pinchas Lapide, who accepted the Resurrection, said "When these peasants, shepherds, and fishermen, who betrayed and denied their master and then failed him miserably, suddenly could be changed overnight into a confident mission society, convinced of salvation and able to work with much more success after Easter than before Easter, then no vision or hallucination is sufficient to explain such a revolutionary transformation."[18] It seems undeniable that the extraordinary transformation could only be explained by an extraordinary event and, in this respect, the Resurrection makes perfect sense. The most influential philosopher of the 20th century, Ludwig Wittgenstein (also Jewish), believed in the Resurrection and said "What inclines even me to believe in Christ's resurrection? … If I am to be REALLY saved, - what I need is CERTAINTY - not wisdom, dreams or speculations - and this certainty is faith."[19]

3	Unique Phenomenon
	It is a matter of historical hard fact that a unique phenomenon emerged in the first century A.D.: the calendaring system of human history itself was transformed into B.C and A.D., i.e., "before" and "after" the genesis of this phenomenon. What we see is a story, a proclamation, a testimony, a call to thought and action that creates a new kind of community. It is a community with its own structure, its own rules and rituals, its raison d'etre. And it is a community that is centered on the life and message, the death and resurrection and the divine identity of a singular individual. Jesus was not simply embedded in the very life of the community but the community believed itself to embody Jesus. They spoke with his authority and acted on his behalf. An astonishing ensemble of evidence bears witness to this phenomenon: documents on the life of Jesus that precede the sacking of Jerusalem in 70 A.D., churches in Rome active by the middle of the first century, liturgies focused on the passion, death and resurrection of Christ with roots in the ancient Jewish worship rituals, creeds and initiation procedures taught during the Roman persecution, teachings from church authorities dating back to the first century, ancient Christian communities started by followers of Jesus that teach the "Gospel truth", writings by Church Fathers going back to the first century.
4	One-on-one Encounter
	Jesus is the only person about whom his followers say that they know him from personal encounter in the present. Nothing similar has even been claimed about any transformational figure in world history starting with their appearance on the public stage. Right from the beginning, Jesus was believed to have been "present" to his followers and this one-on-one encounter has continued over the centuries and in the lived experience of hundreds of millions of people. Take, for instance, the revivalist who claims to personally experience the presence of the Savior or a Mother Teresa who saw Jesus in the poor or the believer who hears Jesus speak to her directly through the Gospels or the missionary in a remote jungle who feels the hand of the Lord in the face of travails and turmoil.

They claim to be *acted on* by a reality external to them and by its very nature such an encounter is self-authenticating and not something susceptible to external criteria. For those who have experienced the encounter, the claim is a rational response to their experience (whether or not an outsider takes the claim at face value). This is not a leap in the dark but a leap to the light. This claim was made from the very beginning of the phenomenon of Jesus and has been historically continuous with its growth. In that respect there is nothing similar in history.

5 Miracles and the Miraculous

Non-Christian historians admit that the historical Jesus, at the very least, worked miracles (or was believed to do so). The miracles attributed to Jesus in the Gospels were not performed to amaze or impress. They were acts of compassion in response to tearful requests. He was no wonder-worker. He was a healer and provider. He gave sight and speech. He cured the lame, the paralyzed, and the leprous. He brought the dead to life. He gave food to the hungry. He did what an infinite lover would do. Moreover, the spread of Christianity was always accompanied by claims of the miraculous. The miracle stories of the Gospels are paralleled by miracle traditions associated with the ministries of all the apostles. And this has been followed by a tidal wave of claims of miracles of every kind. Scholars face the temptation of living entirely in the world of the text. They tend not to realize that the events reported in the text pertain to the real world—let alone to the supernatural realm. Theirs is a different mindset from that of either the primordial Christians or the believers of today: the devout are in touch with the world of the supernatural, and many report a response from the other side. If there is indeed a supernatural impetus behind the worldwide dissemination of the message of Jesus, this would comport well with the claims made about him by his followers. One would almost expect such an impetus.

6 Savior

The problem is that we are sinful—and we need to be saved from our sins. This is a matter of history not theology: the universal awareness of a breach between humanity and the Divine made sacrifice in atonement THE primordial practice of the human race. The problem is that our sin is against God—it is a sin that has led to the current human condition: evil, suffering, death. To make atonement for this sin, to pay the price for this sin, the person who does so must be capable of doing so in terms of making an infinite reparation while also being human. And this reparation must be such as to make heaven possible for us, must cure the evil that is within us, must decisively allow us to go beyond death, must make happiness possible here and now. And all of this must take place in the course of human history because that is the matrix that determines human destiny. And it is all of this that the New Testament writers claimed about Jesus: "You are to name him Jesus, because he will save his people from their sins" (Matt. 1:21). From the very start there was no doubt as to the meaning of the mission of Jesus. "Just as through one transgression condemnation came upon all, so through one righteous act acquittal and life came to all" (Rom. 5:18). The suffering for the sins of humanity that Jesus took on himself was for sins past, present, and future— "Through his suffering, my servant shall justify many, and their guilt he shall bear. He shall take away the sins of many, and win pardon for their offenses" (Isa. 53:11–12). If he was divine and human, then his death was the reparation required: his divine nature sufficed to make the infinite reparation; his human nature made it a truly human act. To understand the possibility of one man taking on the consequences of the actions of other humans, we have only to reflect on the "solidarity" of all humanity in the consequences of sin.

The choices of a father shape and affect his children just as the acts of a head of state affect and involve the nation as a whole. But the same cause-and-effect web that connects negative choices and their consequences also links positive choices with their consequences. And that is why it was possible for Jesus—the new Adam—to be the redeemer of humanity. The liberation from sin offered by Jesus is unprecedented. The philosopher of science Stanley Jaki notes that the writers of the Old Testament "agonized over their sins, over their offenses to God's holiness," but they do not show the same "certainty about having gained forgiveness" as Paul, Peter and John in their epistles. These epistles "go far beyond what is found in" Psalms 51 and 130. "In both there is hope but no certainty that one's sins have been forgiven." The forgiveness and purification Jesus offers is illustrated in the assurance given to Peter "by Jesus that he and the other apostles were all clean after He had washed their feet. There was enough pagan lore in Judaea for the apostles to perceive that in Jesus the divine appeared in a sense infinitely superior to the best which the pagan gods evoked. ... The Incarnate God in whom the Church wanted to keep faith was wholly different from those gods because Jesus himself noted, and most emphatically, that no one could accuse him of any sin."[20]

There are three universal desires: to be absolved of guilt and shame; to love and be loved; to make sense of and cope with suffering. He absolved, he loved, and his suffering gave meaning to all suffering.

7. The Purpose of Life

If death is the end, then none of our actions on earth have any ultimate meaning or point. This is the problem that the philosophers and the sages could not resolve since they themselves were destined for oblivion. If Jesus was truly God incarnate, then we would expect him to not only acknowledge the problem but also to give us a solution. He did both, going right to the heart of the problem: "What profit is there for one to gain the whole world and forfeit his life? What could one give in exchange for his life?" (Mk. 8:36–37). "For whoever wishes to save his life will lose it, but whoever loses his life for my sake and that of the gospel will save it." (Mk. 8:35). "Then the king will say to those on his right, 'Come, you who are blessed by my Father. Inherit the kingdom prepared for you from the foundation of the world' ... And these [the wicked] will go off to eternal punishment, but the righteous to eternal life." (Matt. 25:34, 46). His answer was the only viable one, the one that only God could give: we are called to live forever, and our choices in this life determine our everlasting destiny. To make the wrong choices is to lose it all. Everything matters. Everything is meaningful. Like there are laws of nature, there are laws of human existence: you will die and your life after death (as understood by the human race

	even before Christ) could well be a life of separation from God. But Jesus changed the laws of human existence: through him, you can live with the life of God and live forever with God: this is greater than changing than the laws of nature: it is changing the laws of human existence. This is redemption. This is the Good News.
8	**The Life of God**
	Jesus did not simply speak of the life to come. He had come so that we "might have life and have it more abundantly" (John 10:10) – here and now. In coming as Savior, Jesus invited us all to be filled with the life of God, the Holy Spirit. "As proof that you are children, God sent the Spirit of his Son into our hearts, crying out, 'Abba, Father!'" (Galatians 4:6). Consequently, as the Apostle Paul put it, "We are the offspring of God." (Acts 17:39). Eternity begins here, now for "I live, no longer I, but Christ lives in me." (Galatians 2:20).
9	**The Rendezvous of the Religions. The Convergence of the World-historical Process.**
	All the great pre-Christian religious movements and ideas and rituals—from India to Persia, China to Israel, Greece to Babylon—point to sacrifice and expiation, incarnation and salvation. These themes come to a climax in the life and teaching, the death and resurrection of Jesus. The story of his life and mission seemed to represent the climax and consummation of themes and aspirations articulated and developed in the fundamental matrix of the religions and mythologies that appeared before him. It is almost as if he historically embodied what was mythologically, thematically and prophetically encoded. Thus the story of Jesus and his sacrifice was neither isolated nor parochial. It was, you might say, a story that had already been written on the heart of humankind. Take two examples. The Rig Veda of India (circa. 2000 B.C.), the most ancient and authoritative of the Vedas, has a prophecy of the sacrifice of the mysterious Prajapathi ("Savior of man"), a being who is both divine

and human. As laid out in the Vedic texts, the sacrifice of the God-man Prajapathi was performed by the kings and the priests. It is a sacrifice that is required for the redemption of humanity and only those who accept Prajapathi will be redeemed.

The Vedic texts also lay out the procedures for the sacrifice[4]:

"His hands and legs are to be bound to a yoopa (a wooden pole) causing blood shed" (Brihadaranyaka Upanishad 3.9.28. Ithareya Brahmanam 2:6)
"The sacrificial victim is to be crowned with a crown made of thorny vines" (Rigveda X: 90: 7,15) (Bruhadaranyakopanishad III : 9 : 28)
"None of His bones must be broken." (Yajurveda XXXI. Ithareya Brahmanam 2.6).
"After death, His clothes are to be divided among the officers" (Ithareya Brahmanam)
"Before death he should be given a drink of somarasa [sour wine made of an herb called somalatha]. (Yajur Veda 31. Ithareya Brahmanam)

The Indian thinker Krishnamohan Banerjea comments that "the meaning of *Prajapati* . . . coincides with the meaning of the historical reality Jesus Christ; and that no other person than Jesus of Nazareth has ever appeared in the world claiming the character and position of the self-sacrificing *Prajapati*, half mortal and half immortal."[21]

China too had an ancient tradition of a covenant with God as well as the annual sacrifice of an unblemished victim performed by the emperor. Interestingly, Chinese court records describe an eclipse that took place at the time of the actual death of Christ (since the Chinese capital was five hours to the east of Jerusalem, it was experienced as a solar and a lunar eclipse): "In the day of Gui Hai, of the Jews in terms of monotheism and temple worship; and the

the last day of the month, there was a solar eclipse. [The emperor] avoided the Throne Room, suspended all military activities, and did not handle official business for five days. And he proclaimed, 'My poor character has caused this calamity, that the sun and the moon were veiled. I am fearful and trembling'" Another imperial edict about the same event reads, "'Yin and Yang have mistakenly switched, and the sun and moon were eclipsed. *The sins of all the people are now on one man.* [The emperor] proclaims pardon to all under heaven." The most extraordinary of all the interpretations of that two-thousand year-old event was this commentary in the Record of the Latter Han Dynasty, "Eclipse on the day of Gui Hai, Man from heaven died."[22]

On a natural level, Jesus' coming could not have been better "timed." The spread of Christianity was made possible because of numerous factors: the laws instituted by the Romans (*Pax Romana*) and the roads they built across their far-flung empire; the philosophical treasury bequeathed by the Greeks (deployed in the doctrinal definitions of Christianity) along with the emergence of Greek as a universal language and culture thanks to Alexander the Great (hence the rapid distribution of Greek versions of the New Testament); the theological "purification" ideas of incarnation, sacrifice, and atonement in the major world religions and mythologies. Moreover, the conceptual matrix of monotheism, incarnation, and divine law made possible the birth of modern science (which, in its turn, played a major role in the spread of Christianity). Each one of these developments was essential to the dissemination and assimilation of the Christian message. If God were to take on a human nature it would have to be at some point in history, and it can certainly be argued that if God was incarnate in Jesus the timing was optimal. It should be noted also that 98 percent of all the humans who ever lived have lived after the era of Jesus.

10 — Who is God?

Jesus irrevocably changed the human understanding of God. God is LOVE. The Incarnation of God in Christ is a manifestation to humanity of the inner Being of God. Through Jesus of Nazareth, we see God as Trinity: Three Divine Persons in one Divine Nature ("Triune"): Father, Son and Holy Spirit (neither "Father" nor "Son" should be understood biologically: these are metaphors pointing to an infinite-eternal relationship of giving and receiving). Everything in the existence of Jesus involved the action of the Three Persons. He was the Logos/Son made flesh. He was filled with the Holy Spirit. He was sent by the Father and to see him was to see the Father.

Jesus revealed that "God is Spirit, and those who worship him must worship in Spirit and truth." (John 4: 4). The two primary acts of spirit are knowing and willing: knowing what is true, loving what is good. To say God is Trinity is to say that, as Spirit, God exists, knows and loves infinitely: God as knower and lover, God known, God loved: But there is only ONE God: God the eternally existent infinite Spirit knowing and loving, God in his knowingness, God in his lovingness:

One infinite Mind and Will that exists, knows and loves infinitely and eternally. Note that there can only be Three Persons in the Godhead because infinite Spirit by its nature performs only two acts internal to it: knowing and loving. And thus there can only be God as Knower and Lover (Father), God as Known (Image/Word/Son) and God as Loved (Gift/Holy Spirit). Hence, across diverse cultures and untold ages humanity has recognized God as tri-personal: Being, Knowing, Loving.

The Trinitarian being of God is pre-figured in the religious traditions of India, China, Israel which represent the three main human approaches to God: cyclic-mystical (India); unity-in- multiplicity/harmony (China); historical-linear (Israel). In the Hindu holy books of India,

God is seen as Saccidananda: Being, Knowledge, Bliss. In China we have the ancient Taoist belief in God as the "Three Pure Ones:" "The Universally Honored One of Origin" or "The Celestial Worthy of the Primordial Beginning;" "The Celestial Worthy of the Numinous Treasure" who reveals the scriptures; "The Celestial Worthy of the Way and its Power" or "The Universally Honored One of Virtues." In the Tanakh, the Hebrew Bible, God is described as Father, Word/Wisdom and Spirit/Shekinah. God is called Elohim, a plural noun used in a singular sense to honor the divine majesty. Elohim appears 2,570 times starting with Genesis.

Jesus' revelation also confirmed what reason suggests about God's inner being: God is infinitely perfect and this means the infinite Spirit is perfect love just as it is perfect goodness, knowledge and power. But love implies distinction, otherness. Love is necessarily personal and in fact necessarily inter-personal: it is a relationship between at least Two. Furthermore, love, as we know it, involves not just two but a third who is the fruit of the love between two. Love is fulfilled, manifested in its fruit. For the love of an I and a You to be complete, it must culminate in a third who likewise loves and is loved by both. Lover, beloved, co- beloved. I, Thou, Ours. Father, Son, Holy Spirit. Again: since God is infinite love, there has to be love *within* God. Since God is infinite, this loving, its object and its fruit must likewise be infinite: Three inseparable "centers" that ARE the One. And in what would such love consist? In a giving, receiving and sharing in full of the divine nature, of all that it means to be God. A child receives its human nature with all its powers from its parents as a manifestation and fruit of their love. Likewise, the love within God is a giving, receiving and sharing in full of the divine nature with all its infinite power and glory. It is a love without beginning or end, a LOVE that IS. "Trinity" is not God's proper name. It is simply a way of saying that God is infinite love. To say that God is Trinity is simply to say that God is LOVE.

When connected, these ten data-points paint a big picture A vision emerges from the data, unifying it and making it coherent: that of a divine Person uniting himself to a human nature: Jesus of Nazareth. The

Logos/Word/Son is divine. In the Incarnation, the Logos "acquires" a human body and soul. Thus we have a divine Subject with both a divine nature and a human nature. In his divine nature, he is infinite. In his human nature, he is finite. Nevertheless, in his essential being, the Logos is infinite. But because the human nature is something he has "taken on," he is fully human. Fully human but not merely human.

At this point we should clarify what is meant by talking of God as Trinity and Jesus as God incarnate.

To say that the Godhead is Trinity is to say within the one divine *ousia* ("essence"/"being"/"substance") there are three *hypostases* ("distinct ways of existing"). The words "persons" or "centers" are inadequate ways of translating "hypostases" and it is important to avoid thinking of these terms anthropomorphically when talking about the three ways of existing and the three kinds of relating within the Godhead.

A common misconception about the Incarnation is that of confusing the divine Hypostasis/Person with the mind or soul of the human being (Jesus) through which It acts.

In the Incarnation, the Hypostasis/Person of the infinite-eternal Word of God is the Center of the human soul (intellect, will) and the Center of the Divine Mind and Will.

When acting as the Center of the human mind and will (soul) It can only do what both are capable of (they are finite and limited).

When acting as the Center of the Divine Mind and Will, It can only do what both are capable of (i.e., it cannot be limited).

Incarnation means that a divine Hypostasis/Center acts as the Center of a human mind and will. But this Center is not the human mind or will: it is not the mind or will of Jesus: it is simply the Hypostasis/Center of the infinite-eternal Word of God that acts through the human mind and will of Jesus. Neither the human mind or will of Jesus are divine. They are simply acted on by a divine Hypostasis/Center.

Can the Godhead limit Itself in this fashion? The Godhead limits Itself in creating, conserving and interacting with the world, i.e., the Infinite limits itself by bringing into being and interacting with the finite. This kind of limitation of the Infinite is inevitable and unavoidable and we know it to be the case from everyday experience. The Infinite can therefore just as obviously limit Itself in Incarnation. On the level of ontology (the structure of things), there is no difference between the two limits. Both limits are chosen by the Godhead on behalf of finite beings.

The redemptive sacrifice of Jesus and the forgiveness of sins

For all the reasons cited here, we arrive at the affirmation of Jesus of Nazareth as God incarnate. But this is not all for there is another decisive element. It is the essential link, to which we have alluded, between his divine identity and his self-sacrifice on Calvary.

The sacrificial drive of the human race arose from a primordial awareness of guilt, shame and separation from the Divine. From the start, recorded history is a history of evil. The most ancient human societies have believed that the origin of evil lay in some primordial catastrophe. This insight has been formalized in the doctrine of Original Sin. The teaching of Original Sin simply tells us that evil had its beginning in the abuse of human freedom and that evil once unleashed leaves its mark in every human psyche (an evil streak that is a matter of experience). The fact that evil of any kind erects an insurmountable gulf between us and God is a discovery shared by all religions.

None of the sacrificial rituals of humanity could remove the stain of primordial evil or do away with this insurmountable wall between God and humanity. For, as we have seen, an offense against an infinite Being, no matter how trivial, is an infinite offense. And only an infinite Being can repair the damage thus caused. At the same time the reparation must be made by someone human since the offense came from humanity. Hence the impasse.

This is where the fact of Jesus' identity makes all the difference. He was recognized as a Divine Person who took on a human nature. He had a Divine nature and a human nature and was therefore fully God and fully man. Consequently, his redemptive death was simultaneously a human act and the act of an infinite Person and hence it served as a reparation that was sufficient and final.

This logic is cogently presented by Stanley Jaki:

Sin is "an offense committed against God's holiness which, like any attribute of God's essence, was infinite. ... And since sin demands reparation, the question vividly arose as to what or who could provide a reparation, which had to be of infinite value as long as God's holiness was held to be infinite.

Clearly, man, whose sinful acts offended God, could not provide a proper satisfaction. Man was but a finite being and as such no action of his, however worthwhile, could have an infinite value. ...

All this could be grasped by human reason. But the same reason could not even dream of a means out of the dilemma. The means was decided upon by God himself. ... In order to provide satisfaction for the sins committed by man, God decided to become man, and provide thereby a being who was infinitely holy and yet also finite in his human nature. Such was the gist of the Incarnation. It happened only because man had sinned and because God was infinitely merciful. ...

Being what he was, Christ could offer the perfect sacrifice by sacrificing himself. In him God made man die for men's sins and provide redemption, liberation from sin."[23]

The first Jewish followers of Jesus grasped all this as pointed out by Israel Zolli, the great Hebraic scholar who was the Chief Rabbi of Rome until his Christian baptism in 1944. Zolli held that two key Aramaic phrases – *Talya'* and *'ebhed Yahweh* – tell us how the first Jewish Christians perceived Jesus. This identification is most evident in his final address to his disciples. "In his farewell discourse, He reveals to His disciples the great mystery of His life. ... He is the envoy of the Lord, the Son of the Lord, the Second Person of the Lord, and the very Lord Himself, God. ... At the same time, Jesus identifies Himself with the paschal lamb, saying: 'This is My flesh and this is My blood: eat and drink.' He identifies Himself with the lamb, not only because the paschal sacrifice is also, in part, a symbol of purification, but especially because He had from the beginning the lively concept of being the *'ebhed Yahweh* offered as a lamb. The Son of God, therefore, is also the Lamb of God. Thus, the phrase, 'lamb of God,' arises from the fusion of these two concepts, a fusion fully matured in Christ's soul. Although no language can express the association of the two ideas as perfectly as the Aramaic *Talya'*, the use of the single term 'lamb' is not a mistake. Christ is the lamb sacrificed for the redemption of mankind, He is the *'ebhed Yahweh*, He is the Son of God. By the sacrifice of Himself, Jesus, the paschal lamb, procures deliverance from the slavery of sin (1 et 1:18f), hence the deliverance not of one nation but of the whole world. (John 1:29). ... The connection between these ideas is of the very essence of Christianity."[24]

Moreover, because of who he was, Jesus represents both Israel and humanity. Pimentel points out that "The sin offering was one of the major categories of Levitical sacrifice (Lev. 4). There were many subtypes of sin offerings, the greatest of which was that of the Day of Atonement (Lev. 16). Hebrews 10 describes the paschal sacrifice of Christ as the perfect and all-sufficient sin offering. In the Levitical sin offerings, an animal was killed. As a creature inferior to man, the animal could bear the sins of man in only a symbolic sense, so as to remind the participants of their sin. Such consciousness of sin is good, but it is inadequate to bring about forgiveness of sin (Heb. 10:1-4). Yet, even a man, if chosen at random, could not bear the sins of other men. Only the Davidic Messiah, as covenantal head of Israel, could bear the sin of Israel (cf. Heb. 7:21). Likewise, only the last Adam, as covenantal head of mankind, could bear the sin of all mankind (cf. 1 Cor. 15:45-49). Christ fulfills both of these roles in his Passion, death, and Resurrection, bringing definitive forgiveness of sin, and the Eucharist is an anamnesis of this paschal mystery."[25]

Previews and postscripts of the Eucharist in the history of religions and their significance

The Son of Man, then, it came to be seen, was also the Son of God. He was the Godhead united to human nature. As God-become-man, his teachings and instructions were recognized as nothing less than Divine revelation – "Heaven and earth will pass away, but my words will not pass away." (Matthew 24:35). This was especially true of his revelation of the Divine Life of which even his contemporaries said, "This saying is hard; who can accept it?" (John 6:60).

But so important was the teaching that it too, like its Teacher, is prefigured in religious history. The sacrifice of the God-man, his offering to us of his Divine Life and his perpetual presence in a continuous sacrificial celebration from the rising of the sun to its setting were all previsioned in religious history.

At the same time it should be noted that the Divine Incarnation and the gift of Divine Life are not simply pre-figured in pre-Christian myths and religions but their content is "recycled" or re-furbished in post-Christian belief systems. We find both previews and postscripts. In equal and opposite ways, they testify to the truth of the "original" – the first as intuition and the latter as "copy." Imitation, they say, is the best form of flattery and counterfeits bear witness to "the real thing." On the preview side, we find the truly ancient religions of India, Persia, China and Israel. On the "copy" side are the post-Christian Mithraic mysteries and reformulations of the Dionysian rituals.

Consider the previews.

India first. In *The Hindu* article cited earlier we saw that the Vedic Prajapathi prophecy includes the sacrifice of a pure lamb tied to a pillar and the consumption of its flesh. Its author concludes that, "all these stipulations are fulfilled in Jesus. Jesus is a pure spotless lamb. He is scourged. He is crowned with a coronet of thorns. The soldiers divided his garments though they had to cast lots for his seamless robe. Scriptures say that not a bone of Jesus was broken though the legs of the two thieves beside him were broken. Christ has conquered death and has become victorious. Jesus has instituted the sacrament of his body and blood, the Holy Eucharist for people to receive forever- lasting life."[26]

Then Persia. The Zoroastrians of Persia consumed the haoma plant after the sacrificial ceremony in "anticipation" of that sacrifice "which will make all humans immortal." Of course, as has been pointed out, this is a pre-figuration not a precise description. "The Zoroastrian rite knows nothing of an incarnation of Haoma, of redemptive suffering, of salvation through the forgiveness of sins, or of the glorification and 'deification' of human life through sacramental identification with the One who is both priest and sacrifice. While it may be understood to confer immortality, it is not conceived as the means by which life- giving communion is established between man and God."[27]

Next, the Chinese. The consummation of the unblemished sacrifice on the Altar of Heaven was the consumption of the victim's flesh wherein lay communion with God.

Finally, we have the Israelites with their elaborate system of sacrifice and the partaking of the sacrificial offering and their tradition of the Heavenly Manna and the Bread of the Presence. Most tellingly, they experienced and described what was later to be called divinization.

The previews were followed by postscripts. The mystery religions of Greece, Rome and other Mediterranean societies also celebrated communion with the Divine. But some of the rituals associated with these religions (especially the Roman version of the Mithraic mysteries) arose AFTER the coming of Christ. It can therefore be argued that these ceremonies were "copies" of the increasingly influential Christian liturgy of the Eucharist.

Roger Beck, the best-known contemporary Mithraic scholar points out that the Mithraic mysteries as practiced in the Roman Empire were founded "approximately in the third quarter of the first century A.D." The only available material on these practices comes from this era and not from any earlier period "because, quite simply, the Mysteries did not then exist."[28]

As for the Greek Dionysian rituals, Rene Girard points out that "In the Bacchae, Dionysius plays the role not of victim, but of executioner."[29] Notes Wendy Doniger O'Flaherty, "This would make it a ritual of hatred of the demonic enemy not a ritual of consumption of the beloved god."[30]

These clarifications are important to correct a common misconception. The 19th century anthropologist James Frazer theorized that the myth of a god who died and rose again was the standard story- line of the

Mediterranean mystery religions. His claim was popularized by followers like Joseph Campbell. But this view of the matter has now been decisively refuted by recent scholarship. As J.Z. Smith put it in the *Encylopedia of Religion*, "The category of dying and rising Gods, once a major topic of scholarly investigation, must now be understood to have been largely a misnomer based on imaginative reconstructions and exceedingly late or highly ambiguous texts." It turns out that these stories are a "late third or fourth century [AD] development in the myths and rituals of these deities." [31]

The Mediterranean mystery religions and the Mesoamerican sacrificial rituals of the Mayans, the Aztecs and the Zapotecs were certainly driven by aspirations of participation in the life of the Divine. But there was a striking contrast between these systems, imbued as they often were with unthinkable savagery, and the Way of Jesus. The teaching of Jesus, writes Hugo Rahner, "is a mystery of revelation, a mystery of ethical demands, and a mystery of redemption. It is these three aspects that bring it into such sharp contrast with the piety of the Hellenistic mystery cults."[32] While the mystery religions were do-it- yourself systems of ascent to the Divine, the Christian story centered on "the descent of God and the outpouring of Divine grace."[33] Again the idea of salvation in the mystery religions lay entirely in the natural order. But "in the Christian mystery, the newly granted life lies wholly outside the natural order; it is 'life everlasting', 'a new birth' and 'a seeing of God', and there is not a shred of evidence to suggest that the piety of the cults knew of anything of the kind."[34]

In sum, the descent of the Divine, the salvific Sacrifice and the gift of Divine Life were foreshadowed and prefigured in the most ancient organized religions of the human race, the religions of India, Persia, China and the Israelites. Additionally, after the coming of Christ, there was a concerted effort to re-purpose and re-package Christian teachings and practices in updated versions of the Mediterranean mystery religions. Both movements of the human spirit – the Before and the After – testified to the universal thirst for the Life of God.

The roots of the Eucharist in the life of Israel

The Hebraic "preview" calls for a separate study given the Jewish provenance of the new revelation and its consummation of the Israelite vision. Historically, the Jewish psyche had been shaped by sacrifice and atonement, revelation and messiahship, theophany and divinization. These pivotal themes came to a summum bonum – the supreme good in which all others are included – in the life, teaching, death and resurrection of Jesus the Christ of God.

He is the Suffering Servant portrayed in the Book of Isaiah. He is the Passover Lamb who offers himself up in sacrifice to atone for the sins of his human family. He feeds his flock with the Heavenly Manna that is his very Body. The priests of Israel had exposed the consecrated bread annually to manifest the love of God. Now the bread that is consecrated in accordance with the command to "Do this in memory of me" becomes the Body of God incarnate and is exposed to the faithful as a visible manifestation of the Divine Love. The Todah sacrifice that will never end, the pure and universal sacrifice prophesied by Malachi, is now offered among all nations as the celebration of the Eucharist from the rising of the sun to its setting.

From the outset, *the followers of Jesus recognized that his mission and teaching were to be seen not as a new religion but as the fulfillment of Judaism. Everything about it was sacramental, liturgical, sacrificial as was the Judaism of the Hebrew Bible.* Everything was drama in the Jewish world. So also in the Church that sprang from its womb.

From this vantage point we come to see that the body of belief and practice known as Christianity can only be understood as Judaism fulfilled. In fact the first Apostolic leaders of the Church were all Jewish as were three of the first five Popes. The ecclesiastical structure of bishops and priests that sprang up in the early Church, the format of the ancient liturgies, the architecture of the first churches, the sacraments at the center of spiritual life were Jewish through and through. Charles Hoffman presents the parallels: [35]

Priests of Israel	Priests of the Church
Hereditary. Aaron and his male descendants.	Men who meet the moral, physical, and intellectual requirements of the Church without regard to their genealogical connection.
High Priest selected on the principles of primogeniture. High priest is supreme in authority.	One High Priest only, Jesus Christ, the Son of God. Priest who is Bishop of Rome supreme authority.
High Priest is president of the Sanhedrin, the supreme council of the Jewish people.	Pope (Bishop of Rome) is head of all Ecumenical (world) councils.
High Priest offered principal sacrifices, being only person permitted to enter the Holy of Holies.	All priests offer sacrifices.
Principal sacrifices were bloody offerings.	An unbloody offering a "clean oblation."
Sacrifices offered at but one altar, in the Temple of Jerusalem.	Sacrifices offered on altars in all nations.
Teach and interpret the Law.	Teach and interpret the Law that is still binding and the Gospels.
Teach the Children of Israel the Mosaic ordinances.	Teach what Jesus Christ commanded to all nations.
Seek forgiveness for iniquities by offering a scapegoat laden with the sins of Israel, dispatching it into the wilderness.	Forgive sins in the name of Jesus Christ, by the delegated powers of Christ.
Pray for the people	Pray for the people.

Especially relevant here are the dimensions of the Jewish blueprint that concern the revelation of the Divine Life manifested in the Eucharist. The Sacrifice of Jesus, sacramentally instantiated in the Eucharistic celebration, was the end-point of the sacrifices of Judaism. Michal Hunt has laid out the specific parallels between each Jewish sacrifice and the life of Jesus at http://www.agapebiblestudy.com/charts/Levitical%20Sacrifices%20and%20Offerings%20of%20the%20Old%20Covenant.htm.

In his study of the roots of the Eucharist, Brant Pitre has shown how the central vision of the Jewish experience is embodied in the eucharistic revelation of Jesus. His commentary on the Manna from Heaven and on the "daily bread" of the Lord's Prayer is especially compelling:

> *The whole context of Jesus' bread of life discourse is centered on the Jewish hopes for the coming of a new Moses and the return of the manna from heaven. ....*
>
> From a Jewish perspective, if the Eucharist of Jesus is the new manna from heaven, then it can't be just a symbol. It must be supernatural bread from heaven. As we saw above, in the Old Testament, the old manna of the exodus was no ordinary bread; it was miraculous. That's why the Israelites put it in the Tabernacle with the other miraculous objects: Aaron's rod that budded and the Ten Commandments, written with "the finger of God" (Hebrews 9:4). Again, the Israelites had never seen anything like the manna before. That's why they called it "the bread of angels" (Psalm 78:25). And that's also why later Jewish tradition believed that the manna was a heavenly reality, which existed before the Fall of Adam and Eve and was kept in the heavenly temple until the coming of the Messiah. ...
>
> If a first-century Jew believed that the old manna was supernatural bread from heaven, then could the new manna be just a symbol? If the old manna was the miraculous "food of the angels," could the new manna be just ordinary bread and wine? If so, that would make the old manna *greater* than the new!
>
> In short, *if the old manna of the first exodus was supernatural bread from heaven, then the new manna of the Messiah must also be supernatural bread from heaven.* This is of course exactly what Jesus said in the synagogue at Capernaum… "This is the bread which came down from heaven, not such as the fathers ate and died; he who eats this bread will live for ever" (John 6:58). This is a striking

statement. The only other reference in the Jewish Bible to being able to "eat and live for ever" refers to the fruit of the tree of Life, from which Adam and Eve were driven out (Genesis 3:22)." ...

Bread of the Presence	The Last Supper
Twelve Cakes for Twelve Tribes	Twelve Disciples for Twelve Tribes
Bread and wine of God's Presence	Bread and wine of Jesus' Presence
An "Everlasting Covenant" (diatheke)	A New "Covenant" (diatheke)
As a "Remembrance" (anamnesis)	In "Remembrance" (anamenesis) of Jesus
Offered by High Priest and eaten by Priests	Offered by Jesus and eaten by the disciples
Eaten at the Golden "Table" (trapeza) in the Jerusalem Temple (Exodus 25:23-30; Leviticus 24:5-9)	Jesus' "Table" (trapeza) in the Kingdom of the Father (Luke 22:19-20)

... In light of all this, it's no wonder that when Jesus wanted to leave his disciples with a visible sign of his presence, he chose bread and wine. When he wanted to leave them with a sacrifice to be offered "in remembrance" of him (1 Corinthians 11:24- 25), he used the same elements that the priests in the Tabernacle of Moses had used. When he wanted to give them a sign of the "new covenant" of the new exodus – a sign of his love for them and for "the many" for whom he would die – he gave them the Bread and wine of his Presence. By doing so, he said to them and to everyone for whom he died, "Behold, God's love – behold, my love – for you."[36]

"Bread" is important in other unexpected contexts. Pitre argues that the mysterious word used for "daily" – *epiousios* – in "Give us this day our daily bread" indicates that the bread that is asked for refers to the Eucharist:

The most accurate (and ancient) translation is the one most often overlooked. If we break up the word into its two main parts and just translate it literally, this is what we find: (1) *epi* means "on, upon, or above," and (2) *ousia* means "being, substance, or nature." Put these two together and the meaning seems to be: "Give us this day our *supernatural* bread." Indeed, among some ancient Christian writers, it was very common to translate the Greek word *epiousios* as literally as possible. In perhaps the most famous translation of the Lord's Prayer ever made, in the fourth-century Latin Vulgate, Saint Jerome writes these words: Give us this day our *supersubstantial* bread. (Matthew 6:11)."[37]

The Eucharistic celebration also helps makes sense of the Book of Revelation, one of the most puzzling works in the New Testament. In *The Lamb's Supper*[38], Scott Hahn argues that the Book of Revelation is a descriptive account of the Mass (although it can be legitimately interpreted at other levels as well). This liturgical view of Revelation has been held by Church Fathers from the second to the sixth centuries and various New Testament scholars. In Revelation we see Heaven coming down to earth in the Mass, a vision that is continued in the great Eastern liturgies. The Book of Revelation, we might even venture to say, is a coded rendering of the Discipline of the Secret.

The Eucharist as covenantal climax

The revelation of the manifestation of the Divine Life in the Eucharist is not simply central to the urgency of sacrificial atonement. It is also fundamental to the whole "partnership" agreement – the covenant – between God and humanity. The covenants that began with Adam and Noah and were concretized with Abraham, Moses and David come to a climax in the new covenant of Jesus the Christ, the Messiah of Israel.

The structure and trajectory of the covenants has again been succinctly organized by Michal Hunt at http://www.agapebiblestudy.com/charts/COVENANTS%20OLD%20&%20NEW%20TESTAMENTS.htm.

The covenants lead inexorably to the Divine banquet where the very Life of God is offered to homo sapiens.

Old Covenant	New Covenant
Lamb without blemish offered in sacrifice	The all-holy Lamb of God (Jesus) offered up up in sacrifice
The blood of the lamb preserves the People of God from physical death	The Blood of the Lamb preserves the People of God from spiritual death
Blood of animals offered in sacrifice seals the old covenant	Blood of the Lamb offered in sacrifice seals the new covenant
The Feast of Passover is a commemoration of the first Passover and is to be celebrated by the sacrifice of a lamb and the complete consumption of its flesh	The Lord's Supper is a commemoration of the Last Paschal Meal and is to be celebrated by the unbloody offering of the Lamb and the consumption of Its Flesh
"If, however, someone while in a state of uncleanness eats any of the flesh of a peace offering belonging to the Lord, that person shall be cut off from his people." (Lev 7:20).	"For anyone who eats and drinks without discerning the body, eats and drinks judgment on himself. That is why many among you are ill and infirm, and a considerable number are dying." (I Corinthians 11:29-30)
Bread from heaven preserves the people of Israel in the desert	The Daily Bread from the Father in Heaven gives strength in temptation and deliverance from evil. Jesus is born in Bethlehem which means "House of Bread".
"Regularly on each sabbath day the bread shall be set out before the LORD on behalf of the Israelites by an everlasting covenant. It shall belong to Aaron and his sons, who must eat it in a sacred place, since it is most sacred, his as a perpetual due from the oblations to the LORD." (Leviticus 24:8-9)	*"This is my body, which will be given for* you; do this in memory of me." (Luke 2:19) "They devoted themselves to the teaching of the apostles and to the communal life, to the breaking of the bread and to the prayers." (Acts 2:42).

God is literally present among his People in the Ark of the Covenant which also contained the heavenly manna.	God is literally present among his People in the Body and Blood of the Lord which consummates the New Covenant and which retains the appearance of bread and wine

In his study of the relationship between covenants and sacraments, Scott Hahn highlights the Eucharist's covenantal identity:

> The covenant and the oath: these terms are so closely related that the Bible sometimes uses them synonymously, as when Zechariah speaks of God's "holy covenant, the oath which he swore" (Lk. 1:72). And so the covenant is the oath: and the oath is the covenant. ...
>
> In the sacraments – especially the Mass – the first Christians enacted their oath, and so they renewed their family bond. ... An expert on ancient covenants, [George] Mendenhall demonstrates conclusively that the early church observed the Eucharist – or, better, *swore* the Eucharist – as its covenant oath. Among his many reasons are the following:
>
> "Oaths ... sometimes took the form of non-verbal gestures" and one of the most common oath signs, in Israel and elsewhere, was a meal of bread and wine. The Eucharist, then, provided a covenant ritual familiar to many Semitic peoples at least in appearances.
>
> Most covenants assumed "a ritual identification of persons with the sacrifices" that they offered. ... In the Eucharist, the identification of priest and sacrifice is complete. Jesus declares the bread and wine to be truly his body and blood. ... Mendenhall comments: "By eating and drinking, early Christians were identifying themselves with the person of Jesus, taking Jesus' body and blood into their own bodies."
>
> The Eucharist, then as now, had all the hallmarks of a covenant oath. It is a formal act, an outward sign, that renews a close family relation. It includes a pledge to embody Christ, confirmed by the

traditional word 'Amen'. It includes the customary sentence of life or death, blessing or curse for fulfillment or non-fulfillment.[39]

The Eucharist as a vehicle of the Divine Life

Underlying sacrifice and covenant is the narrative of life found from the commencement of the Hebrew Bible to the end of the New Testament: "Out of the ground the LORD God made grow every tree that was delightful to look at and good for food, with the tree of life in the middle of the garden." (Genesis 2:9). "Then the angel showed me the river of life-giving water ... On either side of the river grew the tree of life." (Revelation 22:1-2)

In fact, on a fundamental level, the pursuit of life lies at the heart of history. Says Zolli, the former chief rabbi of Rome: "The whole of humanity has been fighting against the idea of death ... All of mankind ... has employed every sort of means – magic, rites, sacrifices – everything to overcome inevitable death and to attain the life without end." It is in this light, he continues, that we understand the true meaning of Jesus: "To understand His greatness, to really see Him with the eyes of our understanding, we must recognize Him as the only answer to the fundamental problem of all humanity: not to die, but to live."

This is also how we understand the new rite he established. Zolli continues: "It is Christ who answers humanity's desire for Life. In fact, was it not the whole theme of His teaching: 'I will give the waters of life, the Bread of Life.' ... The rite of blood, the idea of sacrifice is basic to all religious peoples, whether it be expressed by the primitive's 'taboo', the Greek's mystery, or the Jewish sacrifices of the Old Law. ... Blood, red blood, is the universal symbol of Life, the most precious of all man's gifts which he may offer to the Divinity.

...All sacrifices, all rites of blood find their center in this one sacrifice of Christ whose Blood gives Life, eternal Life to the world. ... He is the Physician who will give us the good life we desire, if ... we eat His flesh and drink His blood, and thus have God's life in us."[40]

In this context, we recognize a momentous dimension to Jesus' command to drink his blood. The Hebraic prohibition on consuming blood was directly tied to atonement: "For the life of a creature is in the blood, and I have given it to you to make atonement for yourselves on the altar; it is the blood that makes atonement for one's life. Therefore I say to the Israelites, 'None of you may eat blood, nor may an alien living among you eat blood'" (Leviticus 17:11,12). The atoning death of Jesus replaces the atonement offered through the animal sacrifices of the Temple. It is his blood that atones for our sins. And in drinking his blood, at his express command, we receive his life. Roch Kereszty notes that the Divine identity of Jesus is implicit in the command: "According to the Hebrew understanding, all blood, as the seat and symbol of life (Lev 17:11), belongs to God alone. If a mere human being commanded people to drink his own blood, even symbolically, he would commit the most hideous crime of abusing God's exclusive possession of all lives. Only if Jesus is acting in the awareness of his Divine dignity may he give us a share in his own blood, in his own Divine-human life. Who else but God can give us his own blood, the symbol of his own life, to drink? Thus, if Jesus is not to act as the usurper of God's right, he must be acting as God's Son in the full transcendent sense of the word." [41]

Robert Sungenis observes that the spiritual reason for the Jewish blood prohibition "is that the Jews were under the Old Covenant that did not have the power to grant life. Blood was necessary for sacrifice in order to elicit temporary appeasement from God, but it could not bring life (Romans 7:10). Similarly, after their sin in the Garden of Eden, God forbade Adam and Eve to eat of the tree of life, but permitted them to sacrifice animals to cover their nakedness, a representation of shed blood for their sin. In the New Covenant, Jesus shed His blood for the very purpose of forgiving the sins of Adam and Israel (Matthew 26:28), making it now proper for us to drink the blood of the victim to receive life (John 6:53-58). Similarly, those who are members of the New Covenant will once again eat of the Tree of Life (Revelation 22:2)."[42]

Henry Clay Trumbull, the famous chronicler of the blood covenant rite, considers Jesus' command in the light of the universal understanding of the link between blood and life:

> In the primitive rite of blood-covenanting, men drank of each other's blood, in order that they might have a common life; and

they ate together of a mutually prepared feast, in order that they might evidence and nourish that common life. In the out-reaching of men Godward, for the privileges of a Divine-human inter-union, they poured out the substitute blood of a chosen victim in sacrifice, and they partook of the flesh of that sacrificial victim, in symbolism of sharing the life and the nourishment of Deity. This symbolism was made a reality in Jesus Christ. He was the Seed of Abraham; the fulfillment of the promise, "In Isaac shall thy Seed be called." He was the true Paschal Lamb; the "Lamb without blemish and without spot";—"the Lamb that hath been slain from the foundation of the world." The blood which he yielded, was Life itself. The body which he laid on the altar was the Peace Offering of Completion.

He was here, in the body of his blood and flesh, for the yielding of his blood and the sharing of his flesh, in order to make partakers of his nature whosoever would seek a Divine-human inter-union and a Divine-human inter-communion, through the sacrifice made by him, 'once for all.' …

Here was the covenant of blood; here was the communion feast, in partaking of the flesh of the fitting and accepted sacrifice; — toward which all rite and symbol, and all heart yearning and inspired prophecy, had pointed, in all the ages. Here was the realization of promise and hope and longing, in man's possibility of inter-union with God through a common life — which is oneness of blood; and in man's inter-communion with God, through participation in the blessings of a common table. He who could speak for God here proffered of his own blood, to make those whom he loved of the same nature with himself, and so of the same nature with his God; to bring them into blood-friendship with their God; and he proffered of his own body, to supply them with soul nourishment, in that Bread which came down from God.[43]

Jesus is the Paschal Lamb and to complete the Paschal celebration his followers must eat his Flesh. Without eating his Flesh they cannot receive his Life, the Divine Life. The shedding of blood was so important in the Old Testament sacrifices because blood was symbolic of the life of the animal and its life had to be offered to achieve atonement. In the Great Sacrifice of the new covenant, the Blood of the Paschal Lamb had to be offered to seal this covenant and his Flesh and Blood had to be consumed to receive his Life. The "breaking of bread" became the central act of worship of the Apostles because, as St. Paul said, it was a mystical participation in the Savior's Body and Blood.

Pitre observes that "Jesus knew full well what any first-century Jew would have known: when it came to the Passover, you did not only have to kill the lamb; in order to fulfill God's law, in order to be saved from death, you had to *eat* the lamb. As with the old Passover of the first exodus, so with the new Passover of the Messiah. The main difference between the two is that in the new Passover, the lamb is a *person*, and the blood of redemption is the blood of the Messiah."[44]

Referring to 1 Corinthians 5:7-8 and 1 Corinthians 10:16, he says, "In both of these statements, Paul is referring to the Lord's Supper. In the first quotation, he not only identifies Jesus as the new "Passover lamb" who has been sacrificed. He also bases the celebration of the Eucharistic "feast" on Jesus' identity as the lamb. Perhaps this is why, in the second quotation, Paul can affirm without hesitation that the Eucharist is a real communion in the body and blood of Jesus. For Paul, who sees the Lord's Supper through Jewish eyes, it is nothing less than a new Passover. Christ "the Passover lamb" has been sacrificed; therefore, Christians must keep the new Passover "feast" of his body and blood."[45]

Ultimately it all leads back to Jesus' gift of Life: "Jesus would have known the Law of Moses, and he would have known that the power of his own resurrected "life" – indeed, his "soul" – was in his blood. Therefore, *if the disciples wished to share in the "life" of Jesus' bodily resurrection, then they had to partake of both his body and his blood*. If they wanted a share in the life of his bodily resurrection, then they had to receive his blood, given to them as drink: "Unless you eat the flesh of the Son of man and drink his blood *you have no life in you*; he who eats my flesh and drinks my blood has eternal life, and I will raise him up on the last day" (John 6:54)."[46]

It is clear, then, that the invitation to partake of the Body and Blood of Jesus is a call to live with the Divine Life. And, in this respect, it is the culmination of the saga of divinization that worked its way through the Hebraic dispensation.

The Eucharist as unparalleled parallel

As we have seen, the life of Jesus, his sacrifice on the cross and his gift of Divine life were prefigured in the major pre-Christian religions. But there is good reason for us to call it the unparalleled parallel.

That the Divine Redeemer would be put to death and would rise again is implicitly prophesied in the Jewish and Hindu scriptures. But the actual manner of this resurrection was never specified or detailed.

Secondly, the prophecies and myths of the ancient religions were not presented as historical accounts. Writes Bruce Metzger, "Unlike the deities of the mysteries, who were nebulous figures of an imaginary past, the Divine being whom the Christian worshiped as Lord was known as a real person on earth only a short time before the earliest documents of the New Testament were written. From the earliest times the Christian creed included the affirmation that Jesus 'was crucified under Pontius Pilate.' On the other hand, Plutarch thinks it necessary to warn the priestess Clea against believing that 'any of these tales [concerning Isis and Osiris] actually happened in the manner in which they are related.'"[47]

Third, the relation of God to history and the Universe is pictured in an entirely new light as well described by Robert Sokolowski: "Instead of seeing ourselves as embedded in a world that is simply there, we see ourselves as existing through Divine action. Everything looks different. Salvation is now understood as being achieved by a Divine action that has no parallel in the interventions of the gods described in polytheistic religions. We are saved by the redemptive action of God in Christ, an action that was anticipated by the providential and saving acts of the Old Covenant, an action that sheds light even on the act of Creation, which is now seen as the first of the saving acts of God. The redemptive action of God in Christ is then reenacted in the Eucharists that allow it to permeate, like leaven, the life of the human race spread over all the earth."[48]

Fourth, Jesus established a church that he promised to preserve and to which he entrusted the task of spreading the Word and administering the means of divinization he instituted. St. Paul, the Jewish prophet to the Gentiles, called the church "the pillar and foundation of truth." (1 Timothy 3:15).

Fifth, the central act of this church, at the express command of her Lord, is the Discipline of the Secret otherwise known as "the breaking of the bread," the celebration of the Eucharist, the holy sacrifice of the Mass, the Divine Liturgy. "Eucharist", as we have seen, derives from the Greek "eucharistia" which meant "thanksgiving." From the first century AD, it referred to the liturgical celebration of the Lord's Supper, the transformation of bread and wine into vehicles of the Divine Life. "Mass" derives from the Latin "missa" which was the dismissal given at the end of the celebration ("Ite, missa est": "Go; it is the dismissal.") Eventually, it came to refer to the whole celebration.

The phenomenon as a whole, then, was unparalleled. Nevertheless, it remains a striking fact that eerily precise prefigurations of the Eucharist are found in the major pre-Christian religions and societies: the drama of sacrifice with its invocation of the Divine presence, the partaking of the flesh of the sacrificial animal and the sense of receiving the life of the deity. The parallelism is profound enough to support the idea that God was preparing the minds and psyches of humanity for the coming of the Divine Life. Hence the Eucharist was imaged in the worship and rituals of the human race from the dawn of time. And this in turn helps us realize that every celebration of the Eucharist is a participation in humanity's ritualistically enacted yearnings and aspirations for the Divine Life.

Christianity as THE Mystery Religion

The dimension of the Divine Life draws us back to the mysterious nature of the Eucharistic celebration. The celebration was called the Discipline of the Secret because it was a mystery of the highest order, one that could not be subjected to the risk of desecration or denigration.

In point of fact, there were three fundamental mysteries underlying the order of being unveiled by the Messiah of Israel. First, as we have noted in some detail, was the stunning mystery of the Divine I AM taking on a human nature, what is called the Incarnation. Second was the disclosure of the inner Being of God, of three Persons subsisting in the one infinite-eternal Mind and Will, the revelation of the Trinity, a revelation also pre-figured in the religons of India, China and Israel. And the third was the gift to all of humanity of the Life of God, a participation in the Life of the Triune God.

The revelation of Jesus was thus a revelation of the greatest mysteries – the mystery of the Incarnation; of the dynamic of God's inner being; and of salvation through reception of the Divine Life. Consequently, Christianity, the fulfillment of Judaism, is THE Mystery Religion. This indeed is how her earliest heralds perceived the matter:

> "Thus should one regard us: as servants of Christ and stewards of the mysteries of God." (1Cor 4:1)

> "Yet we do speak a wisdom to those who are mature, but not a wisdom of this age, nor of the rulers of this age who are passing away. Rather, we speak God's wisdom, mysterious, hidden, which God predetermined before the ages for our glory, and which none of the rulers of this age knew; for if they had known it, they would not have crucified the Lord of glory." (1Cor 2:6-8).

> "Brothers, I could not talk to you as spiritual people, but as fleshly people, as infants in Christ. I fed you milk, not solid food, because you were unable to take it. Indeed, you are still not able, even now." (1Cor 3:1-2).

"Mystery," of course, has different meanings in different contexts but in the ancient world it can be thought of in two ways.

First, there were the mystery religions of each Mediterranean region: the cults of Dionysus and Orpheus in Greece, Adonis in Syria, Attis in Asia Minor and Isis in Egypt. They were called mystery religions because of the secrecy surrounding them. The secrecy pertained to arcane beliefs like Pythagoreanism and esoteric rituals like purification ceremonies that were transmitted to an elite group by means of special symbols.

In the Christian dispensation, however, "mystery" concerned ineffable doctrines divinely revealed and mystical acts divinely instituted both of which were to be preserved from profanation. Christianity was on a collision course with the mystery religions not because of the latter's "mystery" but because of their rejection of Divine truth. It has been rightly said that "Christianity's problem with Gnosticism was not that it was a mystery, but that its mystery was heretical."[49]

The mysteries of salvation revealed by God were manifested in physical objects and acts that were external signs of transcendent realities. Baptism, for instance, was, from the start, inextricably linked to the mystery of salvation. Along with other basic salvific acts instituted by Jesus, it was called a sacrament, "sacramentum" (sacred oath) being the Latin translation of the Greek "mysterion." "Pagan Greeks used the term 'mysteries' for ceremonies or rituals that established some kind of connection to a god," writes Stephen Clark. "Greek-speaking Christians," on the other hand, "make use of the term for ceremonies that impart Divine life to us in a special way: ceremonies that include what Western Christians refer to as sacraments."[50]

The greatest of the manifestations of the salvific mystery was the sacred celebration of the Eucharist. As we will see shortly, all of salvation, all of the interaction of heaven and earth, is condensed into a single act: the fateful Passover meal of the Lamb of God, the terrifying sacrifice on Calvary, the Son's ongoing intercession before the Father, the daily bread offered *to us* from Heaven. It is an earthly participation in the life of the Holy Trinity: the infinite-eternal offering of Son to Father and Father to Son in the Love that is the Holy Spirit. It is also, in the consummation of holy communion, a partaking of the Divine Life.

It was this Mystery of Mysteries that was revealed in the first century. It was the end-point of a quest pursued by the wisest, the holiest and the humblest. It was the raison d'être of the rituals and ceremonies of *Homo religiosus*.

It was entirely unexpected, unprecedented and unbelievable. Could "the fullness of deity" indwell a mere man? Could the doors of Heaven be opened to humanity by a disgraceful death at the hands of bloodthirsty savages? Could it be that all of humanity is being invited to freely partake of the Bread of Divine Life, the Elixir of Eternity? "Yes" was the scandalous answer to all three questions. But "yes" was the only plausible explanation of all that took place BEFORE and AFTER.

To deny this Mystery was not possible for all who came to encounter and experience it. As the most precious treasure bestowed on the human species, it had to be preserved and protected in its original authentic splendor in gratitude to God and for the sake of humanity. Over the centuries, it was guarded by the Discipline of the Secret against attempts to "bring it down to earth." Against all odds, every attempt to undermine it, whether through well-intentioned efforts to demystify it or hostile endeavors to eliminate it entirely, came to nought. Nearly two millennia after the revelation of the manifestation of the Divine Life in the Eucharist, the Mystery in all its majesty is proclaimed by the Church instituted by Jesus and ritually realized in liturgies across the world. There is a vocabulary that preserves the depth of its mystery: transubstantiation, Real Presence. There is a body of action that transmits it in its sacral fullness: the Holy Sacrifice of the Mass, the celebration of the Eucharist, the Divine Liturgy. There is a theology built over centuries to articulate the mystery of participating in the Divine Life: divinization, deification, sanctifying grace. Nevertheless we begin and end with the awareness that we are talking here about a Divinely revealed mystery that will always lie beyond human comprehension. But it is a luminous mystery that illuminates all of history. It remains mysterious not because of darkness but through its own excess of light.

SHARE/FOLLOW/LIKE THE PHENOMENON OF THE DESCENT OF THE DIVINE LIFE

Chapter 6

The New Testament, the First Christians and the Fathers of the Church Teach that the Eucharist is the Life Proclaimed by the Book of Life; that It Makes Us "Partakers of the Divine Nature" by Imparting to Us the Life of God; that It is a Participation in Jesus' Once-for-All Sacrifice on Calvary and His Perpetual Intercession before the Father; Testimonies to Its Divine Origin have continued throughout History; and It Draws us into the Eternal Self-Giving of the Holy Trinity

"So, too, it is written, 'The first man, Adam, became a living being,' the last Adam a life-giving spirit.'" (1 Corinthians 15:45).

"Through him was life, and this life was the light of the human race." (John 1:3-4).

"For just as the Father has life in himself, so also he gave to his Son the possession of life in himself." (John 5:26).

"For the bread of God is that which comes down from heaven and gives life to the world." (John 6:33).

"The author of life you put to death, but God raised him from the dead; of this we are witnesses." (Acts 3:15).

> *"If the Spirit of the one who raised Jesus from the dead dwells in you, the one who raised Christ from the dead will give life to your mortal bodies also, through his Spirit that dwells in you." (Romans 8:11).*
>
> *"I have been crucified with Christ; yet I live, no longer I, but Christ lives in me; insofar as I now live in the flesh, I live by faith in the Son of God who has loved me and given himself up for me." (Galatians 2:20-21)*
>
> *"Not by a law expressed in a commandment concerning physical descent but by the power of a life that cannot be destroyed." (Hebrews 7:16).*
>
> *"What was from the beginning, what we have heard, what we have seen with our eyes, what we looked upon and touched with our hands concerns the Word of life – for the life was made visible; we have seen it and testify to it and proclaim to you the eternal life that was with the Father and was made visible to us." (1 John 1:1-2).*
>
> *"And this is the testimony: God gave us eternal life, and this life is in his Son. Whoever possesses the Son has life; whoever does not possess the Son of God does not have life. I write these things to you so that you may know that you have eternal life, you who believe in the name of the Son of God." (1 John 5:11-13).*
>
> *"Sine Dominica esse non possimus. Intermitti Dominicum non potest."*

[We cannot live without the Sunday rite. The Sunday rite will never cease.]

Martyrs in the Diocletian persecution, 304 AD

This is where we have arrived:

- Jesus is the Incarnation of Infinity, a divine Person taking on a human nature.
- He gave up his life to atone for humanity's primordial breach of the moral order so as to liberate us from the bondage of evil.
- The sacred mysteries he instituted, supremely his transformation of lifeless matter into a vehicle of Divine Life, are invitations to partake of the elixir of eternity, to enter a new order of being, to be divinized.

The Divine Life took Flesh and walked among us so that we might partake of this very Flesh and live with its Divine Life. We have been invited to join the Divine Life Social Network.

Earlier we asked: who can possibly believe this? On the one hand, it seems an affront to the human intellect. On the other, it seems too good to be true. But this is the proclamation. This is the claim. This is the invitation.

And even the most skeptical and the incorrigibly cynical cannot deny that, if true, the assertion is stupendously significant for each and every human person. Consequently, its foundations and structure deserve and demand a quick review on our journey from womb to tomb.

The central foundations have been reviewed albeit rapidly:

- The ancient and universal human practice of sacrifice in atonement and the associated quest for the Divine Life
- The promises and prophecies of an all-perfect Redeemer of the human race and the descent of the Divine Life
- The coming of Jesus, his affirmation of his divine identity, his invitation to receive his Divine Life by partaking of his Flesh, his death and resurrection.

Atop these foundations arose a structure that remained faithful to the universal intuitions of sacrifice and Divine Life and the "hard saying" of Jesus concerning his gift of his own Life. Astonishing and perplexing as his bequest of his Flesh and Blood may sound today, they were no less bewildering to his contemporaries. And yet if he was indeed God and man, and if indeed we are destined to live with God and require the Divine Life to fulfill our destiny, then his promise/command makes a strange sort of sense. Who on earth could have made up something so outlandish? The answer is only someone who is not of this world, someone who "came down from heaven" as Jesus said about himself (John 6:38). But his words "connected" with the deepest intuitions of humanity and "explained" the religious practices of the human race precisely because they were all "made for each other." Consequently, those whom he chose, and who came to see him for who he was, preserved and transmitted this mysterious Secret in all its Power and Glory. From its blood-soaked birth to its ascension into earthly glory, from its opulent heyday to its darkest hours, the Church of Christ articulated the Truth, preached the Way and disseminated the Life entrusted to her. We might even say that, on crucial occasions (as we will see), Heaven itself sealed the celebration of the Secret with its stamp of approval.

To grasp the world-picture painted by the Eucharistic proclamation we will consider it from different perspectives:

- ❖ How can we arrive at a credible and authoritative interpretation of the Eucharistic data?
- ❖ The logic of God (theos) – Theo-Logic – underlying the Eucharist
- ❖ The revelation of divinization, of the human transformed by receiving the Divine Life
- ❖ The roots of the Eucharist in Christian experience
- ❖ How the celebration of the Eucharist participates in the once-for-all event that was Calvary
- ❖ Celestial confirmation of the Eucharistic proclamation
- ❖ Participating in the Life of the Holy Trinity

How can we arrive at a credible and authoritative interpretation of the Eucharistic data

We have distinguished "structure" from "foundations" for a reason. Let us return to a question we have already considered: Wherein lies the test of truth in determining the intended meaning of the teachings of Jesus, the principal "foundation" of the Eucharistic celebration? For some it is simply THEIR interpretation of a particular passage of the Old or New Testaments. But this approach is a counsel for chaos. Any biblical verse can be (and has been) interpreted in any number of ways over the ages – sometimes nearly two thousand years after the words were spoken. If the reader's subjective interpretation is the "test of truth" then there is no way to build a coherent, let alone authoritative, body of doctrine. In fact, those who have taken the "subjective interpretation" route have created literally thousands of bodies of belief, each with its own unique twist (and some with competing claims of divine inspiration that cancel each other out). But this means that there is no way to know what Jesus actually meant or intended to teach about anything!

Quite clearly this approach is a dead-end with respect to doctrine but it was not the approach adopted by the first followers of Jesus or their successors. For one thing, they held that the Church founded by Jesus (as depicted in the Gospels) spoke with his authority and under the inspiration of the Spirit of God. But quite independent of the question of the Church, the beliefs and practices of these followers, as codified from the beginning, "speak for themselves" as to what they took to be the teaching of their Master. There was no dissension, dispute or doubt in their midst with regard to the meaning of the essential truths proclaimed by Jesus. These truths and their execution were binding on those who professed to follow him. Chief among these truths was the Discipline of the Secret that was preserved as a precious treasure bequeathed by the Savior himself.

Logically and chronologically, the earliest formulations of Christian doctrine and devotion are authoritative for all who profess the Christian faith. If the first century Christians had it wrong, there is no reason to believe that twenty first century Christians will get it right. Fortunately most contemporary Christians (whatever their ecclesial affiliation) agree on this. For instance, there is a consensus that, at the very least, the first seven Councils of the Church were divinely guided in their interpretation of divine revelation. By extension, the writings of the early Christian thinkers called the Fathers of the Church and the texts of the ancient worship liturgies are beacons of truth. This is so because the writings of these Fathers and the theology of the liturgies were confirmed by the Councils. About the liturgies it has been well said *lex orandi, lex credendi* (the law of prayer is the law of belief).

So now we know where to look for the "structure" built on the primordial proclamation of the descent of the Divine Life: the teachings of the Councils, the writings of the Fathers and the texts of the first liturgies. But there is more. While the Councils, Fathers and liturgies proclaimed what is to be believed and practiced, sages and scholars down the centuries generated a many-splendored tapestry of thought exploring the Mystery. Starting with the primordial faith as their foundation, they wove a wondrous web of axioms and affirmations, insights and inferences.

The logic of God (theos) – Theo-Logic – underlying the Eucharist

Underlying all these productions is a metamorphic vision, the same vision that organically unifies the witness of the world religions, the phenomenon of Jesus and the revelation of the descent of the Divine Life. And it is this vision that we have pointed to from the start: divinization. The offer to live with the life of God. This is the "theo- logic" of the eucharistic elixir of eternity. By "theo-logic" we mean the logic of God (*theos*). The "logic" we are concerned with here is the rationale and purpose of divinization in general and the Eucharist in particular in the context of the divine plan.

We will explore the theo-logic of divinization in different stages. We begin with a reflection on divinization as it is described in the New Testament and the writings of the Fathers. We then consider the primary vehicle of divinization, the Holy Eucharist, as "activated" in the life of the early church and described in the first Councils, liturgies and Church teachings. From this we move to the question of how the eucharistic celebration is linked in real-time with the Last Supper, redemptive sacrifice and heavenly intercession of Jesus. Following that we observe Heaven itself vouching for the veracity of the Eucharistic revelation. And finally we see how the theo-logic of divinization relates to the ultimate social network, the divine Social Network.

The revelation of divinization, of the human transformed by receiving the Divine Life

The revelation of divinization was transmitted through the New Testament, expounded by the Fathers and lived in the liturgies of the Church.

The New Testament

The New Testament begins where the Hebrew Bible left off on the theme of divinization.

With the coming of Jesus, the Messiah of Israel who was "filled with the holy Spirit" (Luke 4:1), the Savior of the human race who incarnated the Kingdom of God, the world entered a new era of the outpouring of the Spirit of God. As Ernst Kasemann put it, "It is the breaking in of a new world of God characterized by the lordship of the Spirit." The New

Testament is, in fact, a narrative of a new divinized state of being to which the entire human race is called.

> "Whoever loves me will keep my word, and my Father will love him, and we will come to him and make our dwelling with him," said Jesus (John 14:23).

> If you are "born again" you will see "the kingdom of God" (John 3:3).

> You are "born not by natural generation nor by human choice nor by a man's decision but of God." (John 1:13).

> "We are the offspring of God," said St. Paul (Acts 17:39).

> Even more significant, "whoever is joined to the Lord becomes one spirit with him." (I Corinthians 6:17).

This new state of being is brought about by the Divinizing Spirit sent by Jesus:

> "For those who are led by the Spirit of God are children of God." (Romans 8:14).

> "As proof that you are children, God sent the spirit of his Son into our hearts, crying out, 'Abba, Father!' So you are no longer a slave but a child, and if a child then also an heir, through God." (Galatians 4:6-7).

> "Do you not know that you are the temple of God, and that the Spirit of God dwells in you?" (1 Corinthians 3:16).

> "Do you not know that your body is a temple of the holy Spirit within you, whom you have from God, and that you are not your own?" (1 Corinthians 6:19-20).

The consummation of this divine blueprint was staggering in its implications, surpassing anything that the human mind could have imagined or desired. Simply put, all humans are invited – but not compelled – "to share in the divine nature." (2 Peter 1:4). God took on a human nature so that humans may take on the divine nature. God "humanized" himself so humans could be divinized. And this divinization is ultimately a participation in the beginningless-endless Love between the Three Persons that is the Life of God.

The Fathers

How do we describe God "indwelling" humanity? As we have seen, the New Testament writings explicitly talk of "sharing in the divine nature." Taking their cue from biblical texts and ancient liturgies, the Fathers of the Church – the think-tank of Christendom – spoke of a new state of being whereby the followers of Christ are divinized or deified.

Shocking as these are, only words like "divinize" and "deify" convey the radical character of what is happening. Once we become temples of the Holy Spirit, receive the life of God and "share" in the divine nature, we are divinized. The Fathers were unanimous in affirming this great mystery of divinization. We quoted St. Athanasius: "For the Son of God became man so that we might become God."[1] Other prominent examples abound:

> St. Irenaeus of Lyons: "The Word of God, Jesus Christ, on account of his great love for mankind, became what we are in order to make us what he is himself."[2]
>
> St. Clement of Alexandria: "The Logos of God became man so that you may learn from man how man may become God."[3]
>
> St Gregory Nazianzen: Christ in Heaven "still pleads even now as Man for my salvation, for He continues to wear the Body which He assumed, until He makes me God by the power of His Incarnation."[4]
>
> St. Cyril of Alexandria: "We have all become partakers of Him, and have Him in ourselves through the Spirit. For this reason we have become partakers of the divine nature."[5]
>
> St. Basil the Great: "Humankind is nothing less than a creature that has received the order to become God."[6]

St. Gregory of Nyssa: "The God who manifested himself mingled himself with our mortal nature in order that by communion with His Godhead humanity might at the same time be deified."[7]

St. Augustine: "For he doth justify, who is just through His own self, and not of another; and he doth deify, who is God through himself, not by the partaking of another. But he that justifies himself deifies, in that by justifying he makes sons of God. 'For he hath given them power to become the sons of God' (John 1:12)."[8]

The Fathers take care to clarify that divinization does not blur the distinction between Infinite and finite, Creator and creature.

St. Maximos: "It is clear that He who became man without sin... will divinize human nature without changing it into the divine nature, and will raise it up for His own sake to the same degree as He lowered himself for man's sake."[9]

St. Augustine: "But this is by grace of adoption and not of the nature of our begetter."[10]

St. Athanasius: "As we by receiving the Spirit, do not lose our own proper substance, so the Lord, when made man for us, and bearing a body, was no less God; for He was not lessened by the envelopment of the body, but rather deified it and rendered it immortal."[11]

There was no doubt as to who did the divinizing: the Holy Spirit. God "gave himself to us through his Spirit," wrote Athanasius, "By the participation of the Spirit, we become communicants in the divine nature. For this reason, those in whom the Spirit dwells are divinized."[12] "Because of our union with the Holy Ghost, we share the divine, incomprehensible nature of God," proclaimed St. Cyril of Jerusalem.[13] Said St. Basil, "The Holy Spirit, being God by nature, ... deifies by grace those who still belong to a nature subject to change."[14]

Divinization is a participation in the life of the Trinity. It is entirely Trinitarian in orientation. By indwelling us, the Holy Spirit makes us more like Jesus so that everything we do glorifies the Father.

Neither Pantheism nor Neo-Polytheism

To clarify again, divinization does not mean that we are now part of God or that we are gods ourselves or that our human nature is replaced with the divine nature. The divinizing action of the Holy Spirit cannot be even remotely compared to ancient or modern pantheism. Neither does it have anything to do with yesterday's polytheism or today's versions of neo-polytheism in which it is held that human beings can become gods.

The revelation of divinization is a definitive rejection of all versions of pantheism and polytheism. In fact, the idea that a creature could be God (or that human beings are gods in embryo) is a blasphemous absurdity and all monotheists have condemned it as such. The infinite transcendence and eternal existence of God makes it simply incoherent if not insane to talk of a human person "becoming" God. The Fathers of East and West explicitly deny that divinization/deification means that we become God as God is God (occasionally they use phrases about men becoming "gods" with the explicit intention of referring to them as deified human beings – and not deities). Unlike pantheists, the Christian says the divinizing action of God enhances one's distinct identity instead of negating it. Unlike neo-polytheists, the Christian affirms that the divine essence of self- existence and infinite perfection belongs only to the one true God.

There are only two "kinds" of being at a fundamental level: the infinite Creator on one side and finite creatures on the other. To the created realm belong pure spirits, pure matter and the union of spirit and matter that is humanity. There is no "in-between" realm made up of things that are half-infinite and half-finite. Thus there is no possibility of there being "gods." You do not become a divinity or a deity. *To be divinized means that a creature receives some of the "qualities" of God's life not that it is transformed into God.* At the same time, the union of Creator and divinized creature is far more intimate than anything envisioned by pantheism. And the empowerment of the divinized creature is far greater than anything dreamt up by neo-polytheism.

The Bigger Picture

Talk about being divinized or living with the Divine Life might seem to imply that God is some kind of an impersonal force that powers you up once you're plugged in. But this is not the case at all. The life of God is Love and love by its very nature is love between persons. To be divinized is to enter into the "Love-Life" of the Triune God.

And to be divinized means to live with the life of God, to be filled with the Holy Spirit, to enter Heaven here and now (to be in Heaven is to be united with God). This is the fundamental insight that makes sense of all the doctrines and devotions of Christendom and, in fact, of Christian experience as a whole. In short, there is a new kind of reality at work in the world, a new "force", a "presence" that acts through certain chosen vehicles. This is the story that drives the biblical narratives.

How divinization relates to what we know of the universe and of human nature, how the Divine Life can be present in a physical vehicle, is a topic that needs to be explored in much greater detail. It is the theme of the next chapter.

Before that we will consider how the dynamic of divinization reached its zenith in the Eucharist. As the sacrament of sacraments, the Eucharist was the primary vehicle of divinization.

"We are deified," noted Athanasius, "By receiving the Body of the Word Himself."[15] "He gives a sharing in the Divine Life by making himself food for those whom he knows and who have received from him the same sensibility and intelligence," writes Maximus the Confessor. "Thus in tasting the food they know with a true knowledge the Lord is good, he who mixes in a divine quality to deify those who eat, since he is and is clearly called bread of life and of strength."[16]

The divinization dimension helps us better understand the conversation of the ancient Councils, Fathers, Church authorities and liturgies concerning the celebration of the Holy Eucharist.

The roots of the Eucharist in Christian experience

The Eucharist was the most visible embodiment of the revelation of divinization. Most visible because it was THE Christian experience.

Codes and Catacombs

The Discipline of the Secret lay at the center of worship in the catacombs of ancient Rome. The Secret was, of course, the celebration of the Eucharist. Surrounded by executioners, scoffers and informants, the community of believers sustained itself on the Bread from Heaven received in the Sunday rite. All communication about the rite had to be in code for fear of ridicule, slander or worse; already there were rumors of cannibalism; and thousands were slaughtered simply for professing their faith. Thus Abericus, a second century bishop, writes "Faith served me as food a Fish from the Spring – large and pure, [it had been] caught by an immaculate Virgin. She constantly offers it to her dearest friends to eat; she likewise possesses the best of wine which she serves for their drink with the bread."[17] Numerous Eucharistic frescoes (some dating back to at least the second century) adorned the catacombs that offered refuge to the persecuted Christians. The favorite image was the miracle of the multiplication of the loaves and fishes. Frequently, the ancient writers explained the need for secrecy by referring to Jesus' admonition: "Do not give what is holy to dogs, or throw your pearls before swine, lest they trample them underfoot, and turn and tear you to pieces." (Matthew 7:6)

Eucharistic Texts from the First and Second Centuries

The centrality of the Eucharistic celebration is amply documented in writings that come down to us from the first and second centuries. Three texts are particularly important: the Didache or Teaching of the Twelve Apostles (of unknown authorship) from the first century; the First Apologia of St. Justin Martyr from the second century; and the letter of St. Ignatius of Antioch to the Smyraeans written in 107 A.D.

Here is an excerpt from the *Didache* on the Eucharistic worship of the early Church:

"But let no one eat or drink of your Eucharist, unless they have been baptized into the name of the Lord; for concerning this also the Lord has said, "Give not that which is holy to the dogs."

"On the Lord's day, when you have been gathered together, break bread and celebrate the Eucharist. But first confess your sins so that your offering may be pure. If anyone has a quarrel with his neighbor, that person should not join you until he has been reconciled. Your sacrifice must not be defiled. In this regard, the Lord has said: In every place and time offer me a pure sacrifice. I am a great king, says the Lord, and my name is great among the nations."[18]

This excerpt from the Didache tells us four key things about the beliefs of the ancient followers of Jesus:

- The Eucharist was the central act of worship on the Lord's Day
- The Eucharist was a sacrifice
- To receive the Eucharist, you must be baptized
- Before receiving the Eucharist, you must confess your sins.

The other well-known description of early worship is found in St. Justin Martyr's *The First Apologia* (written between 147 and 161). Writes St. Justin:

"No one may share the Eucharist with us unless he believes that what we teach is true, unless he is washed in the regenerating waters of baptism for the remission of his sins, and unless he lives in accordance with the principles given us by Christ.

"We do not consume the eucharistic bread and wine as if it were ordinary food and drink, for we have been taught that as Jesus Christ our Savior became a man of flesh and blood by the power of the Word of God, so also the food that our flesh and blood assimilates for its nourishment becomes the flesh and blood of the incarnate Jesus by the power of his own words contained in the prayer of thanksgiving."[19]

Here we see again that the Eucharistic celebration lies at the center of Christian worship and that only the baptized are allowed to receive the Eucharist. Significantly, it is emphasized that the bread and the wine "becomes the flesh and blood of the incarnate Jesus."

In his Epistle to the Smyraeans (107 A.D.), St. Ignatius of Antioch emphasizes the need for a bishop's approval for a Eucharist to be valid:

> "See that ye all follow the bishop, even as Jesus Christ does the Father, and the presbytery as ye would the apostles; and reverence the deacons, as being the institution of God. Let no man do anything connected with the Church without the bishop. Let that be deemed a proper Eucharist, which is [administered] either by the bishop, or by one to whom he has entrusted it. Wherever the bishop shall appear, there let the multitude [of the people] also be; even as, wherever Jesus Christ is, there is the Catholic Church. It is not lawful without the bishop either to baptize or to celebrate a love-feast; but whatsoever he shall approve of, that is also pleasing to God, so that everything that is done may be secure and valid."[20]

Councils

The Councils of the early Church were assemblies of bishops from across the Christian world and representatives of the Pope who were called into session to repudiate deviations from Christian truth and formulate accurate and binding formulations of Christian doctrine. The Councils were called precisely because there were controversies over how Scripture was to be interpreted. The job of the Councils was to determine and define the accurate and authentic interpretation of Scripture. Thus one cannot set Scripture against Council for a Council simply is a way of reading Scripture, a way accepted as authoritative through most of Christian history.

Eucharistic heresies did not appear until the second millennium so no early Church Council had to be called to deal with them. Nevertheless, the Councils left no room for misunderstanding as to the truth of the Eucharist being the Body and Blood of Christ.

Council of Nicaea (325)
"It has come to the knowledge of the holy and great Synod that, in some districts and cities, the deacons administer the Eucharist to the presbyters, whereas neither canon nor custom permits that they who have right to offer should give the Body of Christ to them that do offer. And this also has been made known, that certain deacons now touch the Eucharist even before the bishops. Let all such practices be utterly done away, and let the deacons remain within their own bounds, knowing that they are the ministers of the bishop and the inferiors of the presbyters. Let them receive the Eucharist according to their order, after the presbyters, and let either the bishop or the presbyter administer to them."

Council of Ephesus (431)
"Proclaiming the death, according to the flesh, of the Only- begotten Son of God, that is Jesus Christ, confessing his resurrection from the dead, and his ascension into heaven, we offer the Unbloody Sacrifice in the churches, and so go on to the mystical thanksgivings, and are sanctified, having received his Holy Flesh and the Precious Blood of Christ the Saviour of us all. And not as common flesh do we receive it; God forbid: nor as of a man sanctified and associated with the Word according to the unity of worth, or as having a divine indwelling, *but as truly the Life-giving and very flesh of the Word himself.* For he is the Life according to his nature as God, and when he became united to his Flesh, he made it also to be Life-giving." (Formulated by Cyril of Alexandria, read and ratified at the Council and formally included in its proceedings).

The Second Council of Nicaea (787)
"Never did the Lord or the apostles or the Fathers call the bloodless sacrifice which is offered by the priest an image but the body itself and the blood itself."

Liturgies

The same common theme of physically identifying the Eucharist with Jesus is found in the ancient liturgies of the Church. The earliest Christian liturgy, the liturgy of St. James, proclaims: "Your same all- holy Spirit, Lord, send down on us and on these gifts here set forth, that having come by his holy, good and glorious presence, he may sanctify this bread and make it the holy body of Christ." The ancient Coptic liturgy of St. Mark is just as clear: "And this bread he makes into his Holy Body. Our Lord, God and Saviour Jesus Christ, given for the remission of sins and eternal life to those who shall partake of him. And this cup also, into the precious Blood of his new covenant." The Byzantine Liturgy of St. John Chrysosthom likewise states: "Send down Your Holy Spirit upon us and upon these gifts here presented. And make this bread the precious Body of Your Christ. And that which is in this cup the precious Blood of Your Christ."

The Church Fathers

The Fathers of the Church, East and West, were powerful witnesses to the true presence of Jesus in the Eucharist.

St. Ignatius of Antioch (c. 35 – c.107)
"For there is but one body of our Lord Jesus Christ, and but one cup of union with his blood, and one single altar of sacrifice."[21]

St. Irenaeus of Lyons (c. 130 – c. 200)
We offer to him what belongs to him, as we appropriately recall our fellowship and union and confess the resurrection of flesh and spirit. For as the earthly bread, once it is has received the invocation of God upon it, it is no longer ordinary bread, but the Eucharist, and is made up of two elements, heavenly and earthly, so too our bodies, once they have received the Eucharist, are no longer corruptible, but contain within themselves the hope of resurrection. [22]

St. Ephraem
In your sacraments we welcome you every day and receive you in our bodies. Make us worthy to experience within us the resurrection for which we hope. By the grace of baptism we conceal within our bodies the treasure of your Divine Life. This treasure increases as we eat at the table of your sacraments. Let us rejoice in your grace.[23]

St. Cyril of Jerusalem
So let us partake with the fullest confidence that it is the body and blood of Christ. For his body has been bestowed on you under the figure of bread, and his blood under the figure of wine, so that by partaking of

Christ's body and blood you may become one body and blood with him. This is how we become bearers of Christ ["Christophers"], since His body and blood spreads throughout our limbs; this is how, in the blessed Peter's words, "we become partakers of the divine nature" (2 P 1:4).

Even in the Old Testament there were "Loaves of the Presence," but since they belonged to the old dispensation they have come to an end. But in the New Testament the bread is of heaven and the chalice brings salvation, and they sanctify the soul and the body; for as the bread relates to the body, so the Word harmonizes with the soul.

Do not, then, regard the bread and wine as nothing but bread and wine, for they are the body and blood of Christ as the master Himself has proclaimed. Though your senses suggest otherwise, let faith reassure you.

You have been taught and fully instructed that what seems to be bread is not bread, though it appears to be such to the sense of taste, but the body of Christ; that what seems to be wine is not wine, though the taste would have it so, but the blood of Christ; that David was speaking of this long ago when he said, "Bread strengthens the heart of man that he may make his face glad with oil" (Ps 103: 15). So strengthen your heart by partaking of that spiritual bread, and gladden the face of your soul.[24]

St. Augustine
"That Bread which you see on the altar, having been sanctified by the word of God is the Body of Christ. That chalice, or rather, what is in that chalice, having been sanctified by the word of God, is the Blood of Christ. Through that bread and wine the Lord Christ willed to commend his Body and Blood, which he poured out for us unto the forgiveness of sins."[25]

The Hierarchical Church

The Eucharistic celebration was the fundamental act of the Church from its beginning. As Stanley Jaki writes, "The Church reveals its innermost aspect as something living through an act, whereby it acts out, or re-enacts what Christ commanded the Eleven to do in his memory. They were to take the bread and wine and offer it as he offered his own body and blood in the form of bread and wine at the Last Supper. ... From the first the Church considered itself as being primarily a body which performs that very rite, and from the first it was that rite which separated the Church from any other society including that all-encompassing societal entity, the Roman Empire."[26]

The hierarchical Church, in her role as Teacher, did not have to take corrective action during the first millennium of Christianity because (as we have seen) there was no denial of Eucharistic doctrine at this time. The first departure from the traditional teaching came with Berengarius of Tours in the middle of the eleventh century. His symbolist interpretation was condemned at the Synods of Rome and Vercelli under Pope Leo IX (1049-54) and at the Lateran Synod (1059) under Pope Nicholas II (1058-61). Although Berengarius made a retraction at the latter synod saying "I, Berengarius, .. condemn all heresy, especially that of which I have hitherto been guilty," he continued to propagate his dissenting views.

The prevalence of new deviations from the universal Eucharistic consensus, such as those of the Cathari in the twelfth and thirteenth centuries, led to a clear definition of Eucharistic doctrine at the Fourth Lateran Council in 1215. The Council refined the teaching of earlier Councils and proclaimed, "In this Church Jesus Christ is both priest and sacrifice. In the Sacrament of the Altar, under the species of bread and wine, his Body and Blood are truly contained, the bread having been transubstantiated into his Body and wine into his Blood by divine power."

This doctrine of transubstantiation was not a new teaching. Like the previous Councils it held that during the celebration of the Lord's Supper the reality that was bread and wine becomes an entirely different Reality, namely the Body and Blood of the Risen Lord, all the while leaving in place the physical properties of bread and wine. There was no doubt in the believer's mind from the beginning that this Transformation took place. The only question was how the Transformation should be conceptually described.

Over a period of several centuries the language of Transubstantiation was deployed to provide such a description. But whether or not the Transformation took place was never at issue. Moreover the Transformation Itself remained as much a mystery after the definition of the dogma as it was before.

Once defined as a description of the truth always held by the faithful, the language of Transubstantiation was accepted by virtually all Christians of the time including the Eastern Orthodox. The Orthodox Confession, approved by the Eastern Orthodox Patriarchs of Constantinople, Alexandria, Antioch, and Jerusalem in 1643, affirmed the same teaching: "He is present in the Holy Eucharist, the same Son of God, God and Man, is also on earth by way of TRANSUBSTANTIATION [*kata metousiosis*]. For the SUBSTANCE of the bread is changed into the SUBSTANCE of His holy body, and the SUBSTANCE of the wine into the SUBSTANCE of His precious blood."

We will consider transubstantiation in more detail in the next chapter.

How the celebration of the Eucharist participates in the once-for-all event that was Calvary

The faithful took it as a given that Jesus was truly present in the Eucharist. Now if God is present everywhere, and if Jesus is God, it might be asked how his presence in the Eucharist is different from his presence anywhere else.

We will be addressing the presence of the Divine Life in the Eucharist in the next chapter. But a preliminary sketch should be helpful here.

There are five ways in which God can be present in the world. The first is his presence as Creator, namely the creative power by which he holds all things together at all times (including all who hate or reject him). Second, he is present to us in an intimate fashion when we pray to him. Third, he manifests himself through direct supernatural acts. Fourth, there is the incarnation of God in Jesus Christ who is the "photograph" of God in human terms. Fifth there is his presence to us in divinization, the descent of the Divine Life, which comes to a climax in the Eucharist.

Of course the faithful did not simply say Jesus is present in the Eucharist and leave it at that. Just as important for them were two other indispensable and inescapable truths: the celebration of the Eucharist is a sacrifice and Holy Communion, the reception of the Eucharist, is inextricably linked to the divine scheme of salvation in our lives. It is easy to see why this could not but be the case. If Jesus is present in the Eucharist, and if the Eucharistic celebration is an offering up to the Father of the Body and Blood of Jesus, then this act is by that very fact a sacrifice. And if the Eucharist is a vehicle of Divine Life, then its reception in Holy Communion will divinize the rightly inclined recipient. And salvation is the endpoint of divinization.

But both truths raise further questions: the same Christians who said that the Eucharist is a sacrifice also said that the sacrifice of Jesus on Calvary achieved redemption for the human race "once for all." The epistle to the Hebrews says: "He has no need, as did the high priests, to offer sacrifice day after day, first for his own sins and then for those of the people; he did that once for all when he offered himself." (Hebrews 7:27). "Not that he might offer himself repeatedly, as the high priest enters each year into the sanctuary with blood that is not his own; if that were so, he would have had to suffer repeatedly from the foundation of the world. But now once for all he has appeared at the end of the ages to take away sin by his sacrifice." (Hebrews 9:25-26). This being the case, is the Eucharistic celebration trying to repeat the unrepeatable? And if redemption was achieved "once for all", what is the urgency of divinization? And what about those who do not partake of the Eucharist? These questions need our attention next.

Let us start of by noting that the Fathers, Councils and liturgies were unanimous in their affirmation that the Eucharistic celebration was a sacrifice. J.N.D. Kelly, one of the pre-eminent historians of ancient Christianity, observes that "The Eucharist was also, of course, the great act of worship of the Christians, their sacrifice. The writers and liturgies are unanimous in recognizing it as such."[27]

With regard to the relevant biblical texts and theological truths, interpretation again is the key. The very Epistle of Hebrews that talks of the "once for all" sacrifice emphasizes two other key truths: the danger of falling away and being damned that is faced by the followers of Jesus and the ongoing intercession of Jesus the High Priest before the Father. In fact warnings of redeemed Christians falling away punctuate half the epistle. Most bracing of all is Hebrews 10:26-29: "If we sin deliberately after receiving knowledge of the truth, there no longer remains sacrifice for sins but a fearful prospect of judgment and a flaming fire that is going to consume the adversaries. Anyone who rejects the law of Moses is put to death without pity on the testimony of two or three witnesses. Do you not think that a much worse punishment is due the one who has contempt for the Son of God, considers unclean the covenant-blood by which he was consecrated, and insults the spirit of grace?" In Hebrews 4:4-6 we read: "For it is impossible in the case of those who have once been enlightened and tasted the heavenly gift and shared in the holy Spirit and tasted the good word of God and the powers of the age to come, and then have fallen away, to bring them to repentance again, since they are recrucifying the Son of God for themselves and holding him up to contempt." These warnings directed at baptized Christians are echoed in other epistles. For instance, 2 Peter 2:1 tells us: "There will be false teachers among you, who will introduce destructive heresies and even deny the Master who *ransomed them*, bringing swift destruction on themselves."

But in facing these perilous possibilities, Christians are not left to fend for themselves. "He, because he remains forever, has a priesthood that does not pass away. Therefore, he is always able to save those who approach God through him, since he lives forever to make intercession for them." (Hebrews 7:24-25). This celestial intercession, says Hebrews, involves "better sacrifices": "According to the law almost everything is purified by blood, and without the shedding of blood there is no forgiveness. Therefore, it was necessary for the copies of the heavenly things to be purified by these rites, but the heavenly things themselves by better sacrifices than these. For Christ did not enter into a sanctuary made by hands, a copy of the true one, but heaven itself, that he might now appear before God on our behalf." (Hebrews 9:22-24). In Romans 8:34 we read, "It is Christ ... at the right hand of God who indeed intercedes for us."

So two things are apparent: the "once for all" sacrifice of redemption does not guarantee salvation for anyone and Jesus continues to intercede for humanity in his role as heavenly High Priest. And when these truths are placed alongside the command to continually perform the commemorative sacrifice, we see why the celebration of the Eucharist is urgent and necessary.

For the Eucharist is celebrated in obedience to the command of Jesus himself who said that his followers were to continue making his Sacrifice present before them ("Do this in memory of me"). The early Church faithfully followed this command and the "breaking of the bread" was in fact their fundamental religious ritual as seen in the epistles of St. Paul and the Acts of the Apostles. Moreover, the dread warning against falling away in Hebrews is preceded by an exhortation to participate in the Eucharistic celebration: "We should not stay away from our assembly, as is the custom of some." (Hebrews 10:25). Sungenis points out that "after indicating in verse 25 that some Christians are neglecting the regular assembly (the Church), a dire warning is issued in verse 26 that those who do so are 'deliberately sinning' and that for them 'no sacrifice for sins is left.'"[28] Hebrews 13:10 specifically refers to the reception of the Eucharist: "We have an altar from which those who serve the tabernacle have no right to eat." This signifies that only the baptized can partake of the Eucharist.

The biblical accounts of the intercession of Jesus in Heaven show that there is a distinction between the redemptive offering at Calvary and the application of its benefits that continues to the end of time. Jesus' death on the Cross brought about redemption for humanity once for all by opening the gate of Heaven that had been closed by Original Sin. But entry through this gate is not automatic and hinges on our response to the divine invitation. We receive divine assistance in saying Yes through various means but most of all in the celebration of the Eucharist which is a participation in the sacrifice of Calvary. We emphasize that it is a participation in the sacrifice of Calvary and not a repetition of it. Jesus as God is outside time and his once for all sacrifice is thus "present" eternally. The act of redemption from Original Sin took place once for all on the Cross but the offering up of Jesus to the Father that was the essence of Calvary is made sacramentally and bloodlessly present at the Eucharistic assembly. St. Paul pointedly notes: "The cup of blessing that we bless, is it not a participation in the blood of Christ? The bread that we break, is it not a participation in the body of Christ?" (1Corinthians 10:16). And, as noted, this sacrifice is performed at the express command of Jesus.

The New Testament, in fact, portrays three events relating to the Eucharistic celebration that flow from each other. At the Paschal Meal, Jesus announces his intention to lay down his life in atonement for sin and called on his followers to eat his Flesh and drink his Blood as an actualization of this Event. At Calvary, he executes his intention. And, finally, in Heaven, he continues to intercede for us before the Father.

There is an obvious connection between these three great acts: intention then execution then application. The prophecy of Isaiah speaks of the Servant who is taken as a lamb to its slaughter. The prophetic Book of Revelation shows the Lamb who now reigns in Heaven – but a Lamb who now and forever is a Lamb that has been slain. Each offering of the Lamb subsumes in its reality and significance all that was done before: Calvary subsumes the Paschal Meal and the Intercession in Heaven subsumes both Calvary and the Paschal Meal. Each offering gives meaning to the next: the offering made at the Last Supper shows the purpose of the Passion; and the Passion makes possible the intercession in Heaven.

The Eucharistic celebration in turn brings the offering of Jesus to the Father before us here and now. It is by no means a repetition or a new offering but a bloodless participation in the essence of Calvary which is the Son's self-offering to the Father. In this respect it is a manifestation in earthly terms of the one continuous Act of Offering in Heaven made by the Son before the Father – for the heavenly offering is the Son's perpetual offering of the death on Calvary to the Father. This point has been well made by the great theologian M.J. Scheeben: "By the celebration of the sacrificial act which takes place on this earth, the Church is able to enter directly into union with the heavenly sacrifice Christ offers in the body that is glorified ... The Eucharistic act of sacrifice bears the stamp of immolation consummated on the cross, and reenacts it vividly in its form and power, only so far as in the heavenly holocaust the immolation of the cross is exhibited and offered in God's eternal remembrance, and this remembrance is visibly depicted to us in the separation of the blood from the body in the Eucharist by the difference between the species."[29]

The Son's intercession in Heaven is intended to "apply" the salvific and sanctifying effects of his death for the continued well-being of the human race. The Divine Liturgy, as the earthly manifestation of this heavenly offering, is a vehicle of these very same effects in a localized setting. This understanding of the Eucharistic celebration is reflected in the New Testament, from the Epistles to the Book of Revelation, and in all the great liturgies. The Lord's Supper is a union of heaven and earth for, as St. John Chrysostom said, "We have our victim in heaven, our priest in heaven, our sacrifice in heaven … When you see the Lord sacrificed and lying as an oblation, and the priest standing by the sacrifice and praying, and all things reddened with that precious blood, do you think that you are still among men and standing on earth?"[30]

Eric Mascall spells out the sacramental dimension: "The purpose of a sign is to represent; and the purpose of that particular kind of sign which is a sacrament is to *re*-present, to make present, to effect, that which is represented. … In the sacramental order the Mass contains and communicates the whole redemptive activity of Christ … The Mass is therefore neither a new sacrifice nor a part of the one Sacrifice; it *is* the one Sacrifice in its totality, present under a sign. … It just *is* the sacrifice – sacramentally."[31]

Just as solar energy lamps capture the energy of the sun and provide light for us at night, so also the Eucharistic celebration is a lamp that furnishes us with the light of Calvary. And just as the light from the lamp is a manifestation of the sun's energy so also the Eucharist receives its power from Calvary.

Why do we need this liturgical rendition of the Holy Sacrifice? Because, at the most basic level, both we and the world need it for our very survival. We need it to propitiate God for the sins that we continue to commit against him – Calvary was propitiation for Original Sin, the Eucharistic celebration is propitiation for "actual" sins. The code of conduct in the universe is not restricted to the physical world but applies to the spiritual order as well. Infringements of the laws and principles of the spiritual order bring about consequences as surely as attempts to defy the laws of nature (as when we knowingly place ourselves in front of a speeding bullet or a speeding truck).

"Punishment" for actual sins did not cease with Calvary – this is amply evident in the New Testament, particularly in Hebrews – and it is for this reason that we offer up the Divine Liturgy as propitiation, an offering that is an earthly application of Christ's continual offering of his death on Calvary in Heaven. But it is not simply for propitiation: it is also for spiritual birth and growth and for the application to specific needs of the power of the divine Sacrifice. The universal power of the Sacrifice of Calvary is localized, its effects made locally available.

In Revelation 5:6 we see Jesus as "a lamb that seemed to have been slain." The Victim who was sacrificed on Calvary rose again and was glorified but will always remain a Victim. His continued intercession on our behalf is required and so he continues to intercede for us as remarkably visualized in the Epistles to the Hebrews and the Romans. In celebrating the Eucharist, we not only bring to mind but actually participate in the suffering of the Lamb who was slaughtered. This greatest imaginable tragedy is in its piercing poignance the reverse image of the inexpressible sorrow of sin. The memory of his Passion is to be remembered and re-presented in its reality in the Divine Sacrifice through all of history. Calvary will never be a distant event in the past: it will be offered "from the rising of the sun to its setting" in "every place." (Malachi).

Celestial confirmation of the Eucharistic proclamation

No matter how eloquently it is expounded, the proclamation that the Divine Life becomes present in a physical vehicle is an extraordinary claim. It pushes the human intellect far beyond its credibility comfort zone. This was just as much the case in Jesus' time. In fact many of those who listened to his command to eat his flesh and drink his blood, including several of his followers, left him at that point. But he refused to soften the shock or modify his "hard saying" and was even willing to risk the loss of his Apostles ("Will you also leave me?"). Nonetheless he had prepared the minds and hearts of the multitudes with an extraordinary act: the miracle of the multiplication of the loaves. It is no coincidence that this miracle was performed just before the eucharistic discourse. His followers could not fail to see the connection. Nevertheless many left.

Extraordinarily enough, as if following this pattern set by Jesus, the proclamation of the transformation of bread and wine into an embodiment of the Divine Life was not simply confined to text and ritual. It has also received extraordinary confirmation in phenomena that are naturally inexplicable. The centuries-long proclamation of the miracle that is the

Eucharist has been accompanied by centuries-long and continent-wide Eucharistic miracles.

On various occasions in history, the bread and wine consecrated at Mass have verifiably turned into flesh and blood and, more important, have retained the characteristics of flesh and blood over centuries. These can be observed even today. There is no scientific explanation for these phenomena. Other kinds of eucharistic miracles include preservation of the consecrated Host or Hosts over centuries, Hosts that transcend gravity or other laws of nature, visions of Jesus witnessed by the congregation during the consecration of the Host and lifetime subsistence on the Host alone. In parallel with these phenomena, there have been claims of celestial messages about the Eucharist being delivered to certain individuals.

For reasons of space we cannot review these extraordinary events but numerous works have chronicled and documented their historical basis. Any detailed study of these events cannot but awaken a sense of awe in the face of their profusion, diversity and spontaneity.

Eucharistic miracles have been reported from the days of the catacombs. Tarsicius, a Christian of the third century, was martyred for protecting the Eucharist from desecration; the Eucharist he was carrying is said to have disappeared when he was beaten to death by his persecutors. Referring to other such miracles, St.Cyprian, writing circa 258 A.D., states: "If you do not fear future punishment, at least fear those of the present. How many apostates do we behold who have met an unhappy end? One is struck dumb, another possessed by a demon becomes his own executioner. This one, attempting to communicate [i.e., receive communion] amongst the faithful, is seized by horrible convulsions. That one, striving to open the tabernacle in which the body of the Lord was preserved, sees flames issuing forth." Eucharistic miracles were also described by Church Fathers like St.John Chrysostom (d. 407), who reported that the Eucharist turned to stone when it was consumed by a heretic, St. Gregory of Nazianzus (d. 389) and St. Gregory the Great (d. 604).

Starting with the Miracle of Lanciano in the eighth century, Italy became the single most prominent location for Eucharistic miracles, with miracles reported in every century from the eleventh through the eighteenth. Most of these miracles left tangible footprints available for contemporary inspection. The miracles were not, of course, restricted to Italy. Other significant sites of Eucharistic miracles in the second Christian millennium included France, Germany, Austria, Belgium, Holland, Portugal, Spain, Czechoslovakia and Poland. In the twentieth century, Eucharistic Miracles have been reported in Venezuela, Japan, Germany and the USA.

The greatest of the Eucharistic miracles was that of Lanciano which took place around 700 A.D. A priest wrestling with doubts about the Real Presence of Christ in the Eucharist prayed for faith. During Mass, right after consecration, the eucharistic elements that previously had the appearance of bread and the wine literally became flesh and blood. They retain these characteristics today some 1300 years later. Two distinguished scientists who analyzed the Flesh and the Blood in the 1970'ss and 1980's came to the following conclusions:

The Flesh is real Flesh. The Blood is real Blood.

The Flesh and the Blood belong to the human species.

The Flesh consists of the muscular tissue of the heart.

In the Flesh we see present in section: the myocardium, the endocardium, the vagus nerve and also the left ventricle of the heart for the large thickness of the myocardium.

The Flesh is a "HEART" complete in its essential structure. The Flesh and the Blood have the same blood-type: AB.

In the Blood there were found proteins in the same normal proportions (percentage-wise) as are found in the sero-proteic make-up of the fresh normal blood.

In the Blood there were also found these minerals: chlorides, phosphorus, magnesium, potassium, sodium and calcium.

The preservation of the Flesh and of the Blood, which were left in their natural state for twelve centuries and exposed to the action of atmospheric and biological agents, remains an extraordinary phenomenon.

Eucharistic miracles may be classified under the following categories (for a more detailed description of these miracles, please refer to *God-Fleshed: A Chronicle of the Comings of Christ*):

- Transformation of the Eucharistic Host into flesh
- Appearance of blood on the Host
- Transformation of the consecrated "wine" into blood
- Preservation of the Host or Hosts over centuries
- Host or Hosts that transcend gravity or other laws of nature
- Visions of Jesus witnessed by the congregation during the consecration of the Host
- Lifetime subsistence on the Host

Eucharistic miracles of a "negative" kind include the ability of Satanists to discern the difference between consecrated and unconsecrated hosts.

These miracles can be further classified under the following heads:

- Ancient Eucharistic Miracles with Continuous Contemporary Evidence
- Modern Eucharistic Miracles with Continuous Contemporary Evidence
- Hosts that Transcended the Laws of Nature
- Visions of Jesus during the Mass.

Drilling deeper, the facts that may be deemed indisputable in the historical miracles are these:

- Continued preservation of Hosts that have turned to flesh
- Continued preservation of Hosts with streaks of blood
- Continued preservation of Hosts involved in other supernatural phenomena

Clearly, claims of miracles of the Eucharist cannot be dismissed as hallucinations because the subjects of some of these miracles – Hosts that have turned to flesh – are even today available for tangible observation.

A skeptic could very well admit that the Hosts do indeed continue to mysteriously perdure over such a long period of time but deny that anything else extraordinary took place. It is true that we cannot today prove to the skeptic that the piece of flesh on display today was once a piece of bread. But what is important here is that there is at least one hard and indisputable fact that defies natural explanation: the continued preservation of the Host, the Flesh or the Blood as the case may be. And, while we cannot, by the very nature of the case, replicate the transformation of the Host into flesh, we can point to the continued occurrence of the same kind of phenomenon in the present day.

Like it or not, then, even the skeptics have to go along with two starting points: (a) various Hosts and fragments of flesh have been preserved over long periods of time and (b) reliable reports of the conversion of Hosts into flesh and blood continue to this very day and in certain cases these conversions have been accurately recorded.

That there is something extraordinary about the first starting point, the preservation of Hosts and particles of flesh and blood over centuries, cannot be denied for the following reasons:

- In the case of the flesh, scientific analysis in the main instances has shown that the object in question is human flesh. How this flesh could retain its original characteristics over hundreds of years despite exposure to physical, biological and atmospheric contaminants is inexplicable on a purely natural level.
- In the case of the blood, again scientific analysis has confirmed that we are dealing with human blood – in fact, blood with the sero-proteic make-up of fresh blood and containing all the minerals present in normal blood. It is well known that blood loses its chemical properties within an hour of being shed and blood from a corpse decays almost immediately. In the case of Lanciano, Trani, Santarem, Florence and others, the samples of blood have been preserved for literally hundreds of years – without any preservatives present. This pattern of retaining the external and chemical characteristics of blood is true not just of the drops of blood preserved in their original state but also in those instances – like Daroca and Bolsena - where bloodstains continue to remain

on corporals (the cloth on which the Host and the chalice are placed during Mass).
- Scientific examinations have shown that we are not dealing with fungal or other kinds of growth but of actual flesh or blood as the case may be.
- The preservation of the Hosts is noteworthy because these Hosts are made from unleavened bread which can at best retain its original properties over a period of five to ten years. But the Hosts on display from the various miracles have maintained their original color and remained fresh over centuries – this without being kept in sterile conditions or in an airtight environment. Those that have been chemically analyzed were found to be edible and to retain the same starchy composition as bread. Dr. Siro Grimaldi, a professor of chemistry at the University of Siena and director of the Muncipal Chemical Laboratory, noted that the preservation of the Hosts in Siena represents "a singular phenomenon that inverts the natural law of the conservation of organic material."

This review of the Eucharistic miracles of the past and the present indicates the following:

1. The miracles have taken place over vast stretches of history and geography and it would be imprudent therefore to dismiss them as mere products of cultural conditioning or parochial delusion.
2. Despite the diverse nature of the miracles, all of them are in one way or another compatible with the teaching that the bread and the wine become the Body and the Blood of Christ at consecration. In fact, it might well be said that these miracles testify to the truth of this teaching.

The miracles with continuing contemporary evidence (for instance, human flesh preserved for well over 1,000 years) present us with a set of "hard facts" that demand an adequate explanation. The Eucharist as vehicle of Divine Life seems to be the most comprehensive and coherent explanation of these facts and of the numerous other extraordinary events associated with the history of the Eucharist. What began as a "hard saying" – Jesus' eucharistic proclamation – is now revealed (in terms of religious history, theological rationale and historical events) to be THE "hard fact."

Participating in the Life of the Holy Trinity

In the midst of an intellectual exploration of the Eucharist, it is all too easy to forget its most profound dimension. And even those who come to believe in the presence of the Divine Life in the Eucharist and see the Mass as the Divine Sacrifice can still forget what is most important. The descent of the Divine Life, the gift of the Eucharist, the participation in the sacrifice of Calvary are ultimately a manifestation of the infinite-eternal love of the Godhead. Those who are hesitant to grant the possibility of bread and wine being transformed by Omnipotence into a new reality ignore what is immeasurably more puzzling: why would the all-knowing, all powerful Ground of Being go through all this trouble *for us*? Why bother?

It is this that seems too good to be true, too awe-inspiring to contemplate. But this indeed is what the Church has had the audacity to proclaim through the centuries. The question really is whether we can bring ourselves to believe her message. And that in turn is a question which ultimately comes down to whether or not we recognize Jesus of Nazareth for who he is, God and man. Here we can say, in brief, that only in and through a recognition of Jesus as God and man, Redeemer and Savior, Exorcizer and Divinizer; of his world-changing resurrection from the dead; and of his life-changing promise of eternal life can we make sense of the religious history of humanity, of human history itself and, most important, of human existence.

In coming to see Jesus as God and man we also grasp that God is Trinity, three Persons in one God. There is only one mind and will in God and therefore there is only one God. But this one Mind and Will are exercised by three subjects or centers. Each one of these "centers" or Persons is God because each has the mind and will that is God. The Triune God is an infinite-eternal Act of Love, an Act where the Ground, Fountainhead and Plenitude of all Perfections begets all that it is in an Other thus becoming Father; and the Other receives all that it is from the Father thus becoming Son; and the Love proceeding between Father and Son in the infinitude, intensity and intimacy of its Self-giving is itself a communication of the divine Nature such that it is a Someone, the Spirit. This Act of begetting and receiving and breathing-forth or spirating, of knowing and loving, has no beginning and no end.

The revelation of the Holy Trinity tells us that the mysteries of knowing and loving and reproducing that constitute human experience spring forth from and participate in the infinite-eternal knowing and loving of the divine Being. Every time we think and love, every time we bring a new person into being, we manifest, however imperfectly, the beginningless-endless act of knowing and loving, generating and spirating that is the Trinity. The Triune being of God had already been recognized in embryonic form in the Hindu idea of God as *saccidananda*, being, knowledge and bliss; the Hebraic revelation of God as Wisdom, Torah and Shekinah; and the Chinese Taoist belief in God as a trinity of supreme beings.

The essence of the revelation of Jesus is this: love is the center of being, the most basic "stuff" of reality. Dante's comment about "the love that moves the sun and the other stars" is quite literally true. It is the unconditional love of the Three-in-One that brought the cosmos into being and breathed life into humankind, that redeemed a race in rebellion and unleashed the Life of God in every open heart. Love is truly the energy behind everything.

This Love which is the very Life of the Trinity is with us everywhere and all the time and it is one in which we can participate if we so choose. We know that our choices have consequences. And structures and laws have their place. But unutterably more important is the soul-sundering, heart-breaking, mind-altering all-encompassing awareness that each of us is LOVED at every level, infinitely and eternally, by Love itself. Every thought, every attitude, every word should be suffused by our awareness of the unconditional, unceasing love of the Father who brought us into being, the Son who redeemed us and the Holy Spirit who divinizes us. We should be lost in this love. Every stone, every face, every bird, every plant, everything should sing to us this song of divine Love.

The Life of God is Love and love by its very nature is love between persons. To be divinized then is to enter into the "Love-Life" of the Triune God. The sacrifice on Calvary and the celebration of the Eucharist is an earthly participation in the eternal offering of the Son to the Father in the unity of the Spirit. "The Mass," says Scott Hahn, "is *our participation* in that one sacrifice [of Calvary] and in the eternal life of the Trinity in heaven where the Lamb stands eternally 'as if slain.' How can this be? How can God offer sacrifice? To *whom* could God offer sacrifice? In the Godhead, in heaven, this life-giving love goes on painlessly but eternally. The Father pours out the fullness of Himself; He holds nothing of His divinity back. He eternally fathers the Son. The Father is, above all else, a life-giving lover, and the Son is His perfect image. So what else is the Son but a life-giving lover? And He dynamically images the Father from all eternity, pouring out the life He's received from the Father; He gives that life back to the Father as a perfect expression of thanks and love. That life and love the Son received from the Father and returns to the Father *is* the Holy Spirit." Consequently, "the Mass makes present, in time, what the Son has been doing from all eternity: loving the Father as the Father loves the Son, giving back the gift he received from the Father."[32] The Eucharist is an invitation to enter into this Life of God that is Love.

To be divinized is to be "baptized" into "being-in-love." Nothing can then come between us and the infinite Triune Lover. From Genesis to Revelation, being-in-unconditional-love is the story, the message, the key. In the end, all that matters is the Love that will never let go of us. We have only to open our hearts to the symphony of Love that proceeds from creation through redemption to divinization. It is the Love of the All-Powerful who became the Weakest-of-All to show us the true face of unconditional love. All that matters in this life is to enter into the Triune Life of Love, to be-in-Love without limit, to care for nothing else but Love in all that we think, say and do. This is what it means to join the Divine Life Social Network.

"Faith, hope, love remain, these three: but the greatest of these is love." (1 Corinthians 13:13).

R.A. Varghese

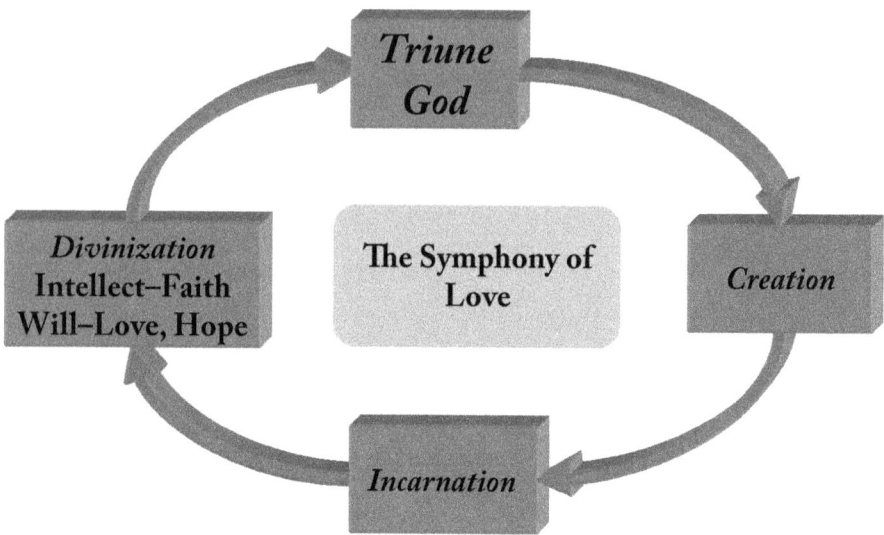

THE "WALL" THAT SITUATES THE DIVINE LIFE SOCIAL NETWORK IN THE HISTORY OF LIFE IN THE UNIVERSE

Chapter 7

The Eucharist is the Climax of the Book of Life that is the Universe as Apparent from the Progressive Elevation of Matter whereby the Hierarchy of Life in the Universe Ascends from Unicellular to Animal to Human Life Culminating in the Descent of the Divine Life

The Theo-Logic of divinization has a counterpart in the Bio(bios=life)-Logic of the history of life in the Universe.

The religious history of humanity, we have seen, is a quest for the Divine Life that culminates in the incarnation of God and the invitation to partake of the Life of God incarnate. Startlingly enough, a different kind of movement towards life is found in the history of the Universe. It is a story of the systematic elevation of matter that begins with the emergence of energy fields, then moves to unicellular life, plant and conscious life and finally arrives at rational self-conscious life. The book of Life that underpins the biblical narratives is thus paralleled by another book of life in the Universe.

The two books, in fact, come together in the Eucharistic celebration which is the transformation of lifeless matter into a vehicle of the Divine Life. In this Eucharistic perspective we see the history of the Universe as a drama of the manifestation of progressively higher forms of life. It began with the creation of matter out of nothing and continued with the elevation of matter into various forms of life. It reaches its climax with a transformation as dramatic as the initial creation out of nothing: namely, the elevation of matter into a vehicle for the highest form of life, the Divine Life that underlies all of creation. Consequently, every instance of the genesis of life – from the cellular level to the creation of the conscious self – is a precursor of this utterly and unfathomably mysterious transmutation, the Gift that is God.

Here we might ask if science has anything relevant to say since it is concerned with the physical history of the Universe. Of course science cannot detect, document or prove the presence of the Divine Life. Not just the Divine Life but the ontological *nature* of life lies beyond the scientific method. Science can quantify and measure. It can map the genome, compute the activity of specific genes, model the descent of species, chronicle the properties of living beings and identify the biochemical precursors, preconditions and entry-points of biological life. But anything that cannot be quantified, anything that is not a quantity, falls outside its purview. And to be a living being, as we shall see, is to be an autonomous, unified, purposive, self-directed agent. And while science can quantify some of the properties of such agents, it cannot tell us how autonomous agency or purposiveness is possible in a universe of undifferentiated matter. Still less can science tell us ANYTHING about the Divine Life, a Life that has no physical property and that transcends all finitude.

Nevertheless, science in the sense of the study of nature has an important role in our inquiry. We are talking about physical objects that are said to undergo a transformation of some kind. Science by its very nature is concerned with the study of the physical. Consequently, scientific models, metaphors, insights and investigations which apply to the physical can surely be deployed in describing changes that take place to the particular physical reality that is our concern here. St. Thomas Aquinas, the great philosophical Doctor of the Eucharist, applied analogies from the science of his day in talking of the Eucharist.

Our exploration of the Eucharist from the standpoint of life will take us down several pathways:

- ❖ How is divinization as it relates to the Eucharist different from other kinds of divinization?
- ❖ Why life provides a model in studying the Eucharist
- ❖ The hierarchy and progression of life
- ❖ The Author of the Book of life
- ❖ The Eucharist is creation out of something
- ❖ Transubstantiation
- ❖ How can bread and wine be transformed into Flesh and Blood?
- ❖ Transubstantiation in the light of the model of life
- ❖ Qualifications and caveats
- ❖ No dimensional presence in the Eucharist
- ❖ What does it mean to receive the Divine Life?

How is divinization as it relates to the Eucharist different from other kinds of divinization?

We have spoken of divinization as the state in which men and women live with the life of God. We have also spoken of the Eucharist and its pre-eminent role as the vehicle of the Divine Life. Baptism and the other sacraments are transmitters of the Divine Life and are therefore divinizing agents. But we do not adore or worship the other sacraments or a divinized human being. The proper response to the Eucharist, however, is worship and adoration because here the only Reality present (whatever be Its "appearance") is the Divine.

This leads to an immediate array of questions: What is PHYSICALLY supposed to take place at the consecration of the Eucharist and how is this to be understood in the context of the scientific account of the universe and life? What does it mean to say that bread and wine are transformed into the Flesh and Blood of God incarnate? How are we to understand the idea of one reality changing into a radically different reality without any change of appearance? How is this transformation brought about? In what sense is God present in the Eucharist? What does it mean to say that we "receive" the Divine Life?

At least some of these questions partially concern events and objects that we can touch, see, feel and taste. Anything we say about such tangible things ipso facto falls within the purview of science. But the transformational claims being made about the Eucharist relate to what is intangible. Analogies from science may be useful in understanding these claims and in making clarifications and distinctions. But the claims of Eucharistic transformation, strictly speaking, fall outside science since science can only deal with the tangible. As a matter of fact, even in the entirely natural realm there are undeniable intangible realities that cannot be described or explained by science. These include life, consciousness, thought and the human self. And it is precisely a consideration of these realities that can help us better understand the mystery of the Divine Life.

Why life provides a model in studying the Eucharist

In the celebration of the Eucharist, bread and wine change into the Body and Blood of Christ at the moment of consecration. The traditional description of this change is the doctrine of Transubstantiation – the substance of the bread and wine are changed but not its appearances. Here we will explore a new model drawn from contemporary experience to describe the mystery of this dramatic change. We are trying not to replace the language of Transubstantiation but to understand its truth in the context of another dimension – that of life at all levels. Life is, in fact, a fitting model. If the Eucharist is a manifestation of the Divine Life, then the ways in which other forms of life manifest themselves will be at least distantly analogous to it. These analogies, in turn, could help us better describe what is taking place in the Eucharistic transformation. A description is not an explanation, of course, and neither the doctrine of Transubstantiation nor the version of it presented here diminish, in any respect, the depth of the mystery involved.

The emphasis on the Eucharist as the vehicle of Divine Life mirrors the emphasis that Jesus placed both on his identity as Divine Life incarnate and the urgency of our receiving this Life: "I am the way and the truth and the *life*. No one comes to the Father except through me." (John 14:6) "Just as the Father has life in himself, so also he gave to his Son the possession of *life* in himself." (John 5:26). "I am the bread of *life*" (John 6:48). "Whoever eats my flesh and drinks my blood has eternal *life*." (6:54). "Just as the living

Father sent me and I have *life* because of the Father, so also the one who feeds on me will have *life* because of me." (6:57). "I come so that they might have *life* and have it more abundantly." (John 10:10).

Here, as previously emphasized, we see that (a) Jesus not only has the Divine Life but IS the Divine Life incarnate (b) our eternal life depends on our living with his Divine Life and (c) to receive his Divine Life one must eat the flesh and drink the blood of "the bread of life." The focus on the Eucharist as the vehicle of Divine Life is important, above all, because the whole point of receiving communion is to receive the Divine Life, to be "partakers of the divine nature."

We have observed that there is a hierarchy of life in the universe and each one of the major kinds of life represents a quantum leap over a lower kind, for instance the bacterium vs. the butterfly vs. the human person. The origins of certain new dimensions in a higher kind of life cannot be explained by a study of the lower kind. The consciousness of a chimpanzee is qualitatively distinct from the stimulus-response operations of a bacterium. Nevertheless, they all use the same substratum of matter.

The Hierarchy and Progression of Life

Let us start with a deceptively simple question: what is life?

The scientist defines "life" in terms of the capabilities of living beings: a self-sustained chemical system, a self-organizing matrix, self-reproducing matter capable of evolution, something capable of ingestion, excretion, metabolism, motion, homeostasis and growth. But these are (important as they are) simply physico-chemical structure and function descriptions. They do not address the fundamental nature of the beings with these physico-chemical properties.

To begin with there is no such thing as "life." There are living beings. What does it mean for a being to be alive apart from the obvious physico-chemical attributes? Several things can be said in blueprinting the nature of living beings:

- Each and every living being acts or is capable of action; each has powers and harnesses energy.

- Each such being is the unified source and center of all its actions: it is an agent.
- These agents are capable of surviving and acting independently and are therefore autonomous.
- The actions of the agents are in some fashion driven by goals (nourishment for instance) and consequently they are goal-seeking.
- They can reproduce themselves and thus they are self- replicating.
- The biological processes underlying the actions of the agents are driven by an interplay between chemistry and codes, rules and information.
- In brief, living beings are goal-seeking, self-replicating, unified, information-processing autonomous agents with specific powers.

Many scientists seem not to have grasped these dimensions of being alive. While the last hundred years have seen no shortage of speculation, no scientist has a conclusive answer even on a physico- chemical level as to the origin of life. Prominent scientists have forcefully highlighted this quandary as illustrated in the Appendix.

Just as mysterious is the origin of conscious life: a new kind of living being that is conscious of its environment. We are conscious and conscious that we are conscious. Our conscious experience includes sensations, memories, images, concepts, intentions and choices. There are two hard facts that indicate the non-physical nature of conscious experience:

- In terms of how we experience them, conscious phenomena are qualitatively distinct from anything physical, anything that can be physically observed or described. Sensations and perceptions have no size or shape, no physical characteristics whatsoever.
- In terms of scientific investigation, it is clear that there is nothing in the brain that has any property of consciousness. Consciousness cannot even be described in scientific terms.

Now how is it the case that consciousness exists? Certainly none of the known laws of matter breathe a word about it. Consciousness cannot be measured, quantified or mathematically modeled and therefore is not scientifically treatable. Science can neither describe consciousness nor explain the origin of conscious life.

The most basic form of consciousness – eyesight, visual consciousness – emerged suddenly. Fully functional eyes appeared right at the beginning of the Cambrian explosion, the relatively short time frame some 540 million years ago when most of the major phyla emerged. The philosopher of science Sir Karl Popper remarked that the emergence of consciousness in the animal kingdom is perhaps as great a mystery as the origin of life.

With the advent of the human person, a new kind of life emerges: rational, self-conscious life. How did language and conceptual thought, the touchstone of rationality, arise? Language is a system of codes that conveys meaning through symbols. The activities of coding and decoding, of seeing meaning, are irreducibly immaterial. Syntactical language is unique to human beings, found even in ancient civilizations and instinctively mastered by children at a very young age. But scientists cannot explain the origin of language or the jump from primitive to syntactical language. This inexplicable structure, again, seems to have appeared as is, out of the blue, with no forerunners.

The unbridgeable gulf separating the human person from other animals was highlighted in *Scientific American* article by the biologist Marc Hauser. Hauser notes that Darwin's idea of a continuity of mind between humans and other species is now passé and it is now understood that there is "a profound gap" between the human intellect and that of other animals. He concludes that "our mind is very different from that of even our closest primate relatives and that we do not know much about how that difference came to be."[1]

Equally inexplicable is the nature and origin of the "I." What is most obvious in my everyday experience is the fact that I do experience things – and that this "I" which does the experiencing exists and that its experiences are "my" experiences. Everything else is something that I describe or experience. "I" am that which does the describing and the experiencing. But this "I" cannot be described or experienced except as the radically mysterious reality that unifies my experiences, drives my actions and thinks my thoughts. You cannot reduce it to anything simpler or more basic. Nor can you deny it. It is the "I" that makes me inevitably think and speak with the first person perspective: *my* body, *my* thoughts, *my* attitude. Since, as Andrew Ross puts it, "science is built from a third-person perspective," it cannot describe the existence of a first person perspective: "*my* experience remains unexplained."[2] In short it cannot explain the origin of the self.

The existence of the self is especially apparent at a biological level. Every one of the tens of thousands of molecules constituting each one of our neurons is changed approximately 10,000 times in a normal life-span. In fact, it is not just our neurons but every cell in our body that is regularly replaced. But despite the constant flux at the neuronal and other levels something remains the same – or we could not even continue reading just this sentence! Individual brain cells are just as incapable as the chips in a computer to serve as a self. So where did the self come from?

The Author of the Book of Life

The upshot is that the existence of any kind of life is a profound mystery. But it is a mystery that illuminates the greater mystery yet that we are considering here – the appearance of the Divine Life in human history. Here a consideration of the hierarchy of life is relevant:

- Matter (mass/energy)
- Cellular life – incorporates matter
- Plant life – incorporates matter and cellular life
- Animal life – incorporates matter, cellular life and includes perceptual consciousness and communication
- Human life – incorporates all of the above and includes conceptual thought and communication, freewill, persistence of identity over time (despite continuous physical change) and the consciousness of the self
- Angelic life – pure conceptual thought and will
- The Divine Life – the infinite self-existent Energy, Goodness, Love that created all other forms of life and holds them in being

This hierarchy can also be considered from the standpoint of the progressive elevation of matter:

THE PROGRESSIVE ELEVATION OF MATTER

Eucharist – matter elevated into a vehicle of the Divine Life by the Man who was God

Human life – matter with self-consciousness, conceptual thought, freewill, purpose

Animal life – matter with perceptual consciousness, locomotion

Plant life – matter with photosynthesis, replication through meiosis/mitosis

Prokaryotic Life (bacteria) – matter with primitive life, replication by fission - also *Archae*

Matter – lifeless (mass-energy)

The Divine Life – from which flows all life – always existed. Angelic life (according to the testimony of the world religions) preceded all other created life. Biological life is remarkable in its own way. The origin of even the most elementary form of biological life is inexplicable. We know without any shadow of doubt that even given a trillion years a rock or a cloud of gas cannot suddenly come to life, i.e., become an end-directed autonomous agent: garbage in, garbage out. Moreover, the appearance of each kind of biological life involved a quantum leap from the previous kind (e.g., bacterial to animal life). These leaps are not explicable or comprehensible in terms of physics and chemistry since they involve phenomena such as consciousness that have no physical attributes.

So how did the various forms of life originate? It seems obvious from the considerations laid out here that life, consciousness, mind and the self can only come from a Source that is living, conscious and thinking. If we are centers of consciousness and thought who are able to know and love and intend and execute, there is no way that such centers could come to be from something that is itself incapable of all these activities. It is simply inconceivable that any material process or field can generate agents who think and act. Matter cannot produce conceptions and perceptions. A force field does not plan or think. So at the level of reason and everyday experience, we become immediately aware that the world of living, conscious, thinking beings has to originate from a living Source. Many of the greatest scientists of all time, from Newton to Einstein to Heisenberg, found it inconceivable that a purely material matrix, formless and randomized, can generate undeniable intelligence. They held that the laws of nature points to an Intelligence that has no limitation, "a superior mind" as Einstein put it.

The Nobel winning biologist George Wald once stated that "we choose to believe the impossible: that life arose spontaneously by chance." In later years he issued a retraction and went on to say that "mind, rather than emerging as a late outgrowth in the evolution of life, has existed always as the matrix, the source and condition of physical reality – that the stuff of which physical reality is constructed is mind-stuff. It is mind that has composed a physical universe that breeds life, and so eventually evolves creatures that know and create."[3]

The brain scientist Sir John Eccles, another Nobelist, affirmed that "the only certainty we have is that we exist as unique self-conscious beings" and that "the conscious self" is "a divine creation."[4]

With all these data-points in mind, we can now draw some conclusions about the manifestations of life in the universe:

- ❖ All forms of life operate on the exact same physical substrate. Every living being is "made up" of quantum fields that are not different in any way. Physically speaking then there is no fundamental difference between non-living and any kind of living matter.
- ❖ To say that something is alive is to say its matter is organized in a certain fashion and that it has certain additional attributes that could not have been generated from matter per se.
- ❖ There is a hierarchy of living beings, this hierarchy being determined by certain intangible and yet real attributes: from mere autonomous agency upward to awareness and thence to abstraction.

❖ No physical inspection of a living being will show us "life" or "consciousness" or "rationality". We know that something is alive or conscious or thinking from its actions.

❖ All life comes from the Author of life.

When we turn to the manifestation of Divine Life in the universe, we will see that the various kinds of creaturely life are dim precursors of the grand finale. But if the origin of every terrestrial kind of life is a mystery, the descent of the Divine Life is infinitely more mysterious.

The Eucharist is Creation "Out of Something"

From the earliest times, the Fathers of the Church recognized that the transformation of bread and wine into the Body and Blood of Christ was not just another miracle. Remarkably, the closest analogy they could bring to bear in describing this event was the creation of the Universe (in both its physical and non-physical dimensions) from nothing. Both events represented changes of the most fundamental nature. While one described the coming to be of natural reality as a whole, the other was concerned with the transformation of the natural into the supranatural. Paradoxically, the latter transformation did not involve any change of appearance. The natural becomes the supranatural while retaining the appearance of the natural (and here there is an analogy – but only an analogy – in terms of identity of appearance between a living being and a non-living replica).

For our purposes here, these two ontologically fundamental miracles of nature may be described as "*Creation out of nothing*" i.e., "*Creatio ex nihilo*" and "*Creation out of something.*"

> *Creation out of nothing (Creatio ex nihilo)* – creation of physical and non-physical reality as a whole out of nothing
>
> *Creation out of something* – transformation of an existing physical reality into a pre-existing supranatural reality while retaining the appearances of the physical reality

In creation out of something, the Event involved is a transformation of something already existing but a transformation so fundamental that its nearest analogy is creation of something out of nothing. "Creation" is used because something that was previously not present is now here and we say "out of something" because this new Presence comes through a transformation. The mystery of this transformation lies not just in the fact that one thing changes totally into another but in What it changes into.

Both acts of creation involve God. Both are continuous acts – Creatio ex nihilo, the creation of the Universe out of nothing, involves God continuing to hold all things in being at every instant; and Creation out of something takes place at every Mass. Both acts, by their very nature, cannot be scientifically proved or disproved. Both acts are believed on the basis of divine authority and both acts make sense of a wide variety of phenomena.

Transubstantiation

In talking of the paradigm of *Creation out of something* – of consecration as the transformation of non-living matter into a vehicle of the Divine Life – we are inevitably led to the traditional teaching of Transubstantiation. The paradigm of *Creation out of something* can only be understood in the context of the basic insight so powerfully expressed by the concept of Transubstantiation.

When Jesus said "This is my body … This is my blood," he meant his words to be taken literally. That there is a Change in the bread and the wine upon the invocation of the Holy Spirit and the words of consecration uttered by Jesus speaking through the person of his priest has always been accepted among his followers. That the Change involves the true indwelling, the actual Presence of God in what was once bread and wine was also widely and fervently professed by the faithful. As we have seen, the Second Council of Nicaea (787), one of the Seven Ecumenical Councils accepted by all Christians, taught that the transformation of bread and wine into body and blood was literal not symbolic: "Never did the Lord or the apostles or the Fathers call the bloodless sacrifice which is offered by the priest an image but the body itself and the blood itself." (Here Nicaea echoes the earlier Council of Ephesus held in 431.) The Fourth Lateran Council (1215) refined this teaching further in the doctrine of transubstantiation which was affirmed by the Orthodox Confession (1643).

But accepting the fact of the Change embodied in the doctrine of transubstantiation is one thing. It is quite another thing to describe what we mean when we talk of such a Change and try to explain how it is possible for this Change to take place. The idea of transubstantiation was introduced precisely in order to clarify and magnify the nature of the Change without pretending to make it any less mysterious.

The essence of the doctrine of Transubstantiation is the following:

- in any and every object in the world, there is a distinction between the object's properties and qualities and the physical substrate, or substance, in which these properties inhere and that endures over a period of time;
- the qualities and properties of an object (color, size, etc.) are part of the object but cannot exist independently of its physical substrate (the redness of a brick cannot exist independently of the brick);
- although more "independent" than its properties, the substrate of any and every object ultimately derives from and is constantly dependent for its continued existence on the creative action of God;
- God, Who has made every object out of nothing and Who keeps it in existence as the specific being that it is with its particular substrate and properties, can change a given object into a wholly different kind of being by changing its physical substrate while allowing it to retain the properties of the original being.

As applied to the Eucharist, when the bread and the wine are consecrated at Mass, a change of physical substrate or substance, appropriately called "transubstantiation," takes place whereby these now become the substance of the Body and Blood of Christ while still retaining the properties or appearances of bread and wine.

The genius of St. Thomas Aquinas was to locate this transformation within the context of the creative activity of God and each object's existence as a finite participation in God's infinite Act of Being. Only an awareness of the mystery of the entire and constant dependence of each object on God both for its existence and its existence with the kind of physical substrate and properties that it has will prepare our minds for the greater mystery of Transubstantiation.

Ultimately, the description of the whole Event in terms of substance and appearances is not the issue. The truth being taught is that the reality that was bread and wine becomes an entirely different Reality, namely the Body and Blood of the Risen Lord, all the while leaving in place the physical properties of bread and wine. Just as the same reality endures through different appearances in the metamorphosis of a caterpillar into a butterfly, in the case of the Eucharist the same appearances endure through different realities.

The idea of a differentiation between a reality and its appearances is more plausible today since it is generally accepted that there are differentiations even at the level of appearances – for instance between the quantum and the classical realms, between mass and energy, between the virtual environments of cyberspace and the real world, between hardware and software. In taking the creation of life as an analogy of the Change that takes place at Transubstantiation, we might be able to clarify some of the more common misconceptions about this doctrine.

To grasp the idea of *Creation out of something*, we return to the model of life. It is surely significant that matter is involved in every instance of the creation of life in this world. Because we are creatures of flesh and blood, we have to touch, see and smell life at all its levels to understand it and work with it. This need is met in the supreme instance of the appearance of a new kind of life in the world: it is a creative act whereby matter is transformed into that which "contains" the pre-existing Life of God while continuing to manifest the characteristics of matter. And just as God works through created agents in the creation of new life, so too in the Creation out of something that is the celebration of the Eucharist he works through human agents endowed with the required supernatural authority.

If someone were to ask what there is that is different about the Host before and after consecration, the answer, in a word, is the Life that is now present in it. The Eucharist pulsates, literally explodes with the infinite

Energy of the Divine Life. But this Energy can be experienced only by the soul because it is literally soul-food.

In saying that the presence of the Divine Life will be apparent only to the soul, we are not suggesting that the resultant experience is simply a matter of feelings or abstractions. St. Thomas notes that the sacrament of the Eucharist has the appearance of food and drink because it does for the soul what bread and wine do for the body: it sustains, builds up, restores. Reception of the Eucharist *can* transform us at the very foundations of our being, cleanse us in the most profound sense, strengthen character as we confront choices at every instant and give direction and momentum in our daily voyage to the divine. We say *can* because the explosion cannot take place without the critical mass or a chain reaction that only we can provide. The Energy that is released is, of course, not physical energy but it is the Energy that holds all things in being.

To perceive and receive the Divine Life our hearts must want It, our minds must have at least a dim recognition of Who is present and our wills must be at least minimally turned to God and not against Him. The Eucharist has no effect on a soul hardened in deadly sin for the same reason that food given to a corpse does not energize it. "Mortal" sin like a "mortal" wound destroys life. But the Divine Life that leaves the soul in mortal sin will return to it if there is repentance, reparation and recourse to the sacrament of reconciliation. And each instance of the physical reception of the Eucharist, if accompanied by a receptivity of the soul, replenishes and intensifies the Divine Life already present in us.

How Can Bread and Wine be Transformed into *Flesh and Blood?*

What sense does it make to say that what was once bread and wine is now the Body and Blood of Jesus? In particular, how can we say that this is the case given that what we perceive after consecration very noticeably has the properties of bread and wine?

To begin with, we should look at the physical facts of the matter. How do bread and wine physically differ from "Body" and "Blood"? Obviously they have different observable properties — "appearances" or empirical "signs" if you will — such as color, taste and the like. Remarkably, however, at the subatomic, quantum level there is no physical difference between any one of these realities. The Israeli scientist Gerald Schroeder explains the essential sameness of all that is physical: "In one mix of protons, neutrons and electrons I get a grain of sand. I take the same protons, neutrons and electrons, put them together in a different mix and get a brain that can record facts, produce emotions, and from which emerges a mind that integrates those facts and emotions and experiences that integration. It's the same protons, neutrons and electrons. They had no face lift yet one seems passive while the other is dynamically alive."[5] In brief, all physical objects — be they bread, wine, body or blood — are made up of the same essential constituents at the most basic level, at the fundamental level of "appearances."

Nevertheless there is one instance in which a given set of protons, neutrons and electrons is "transformed" into something entirely and qualitatively different while still remaining physically the same. We are so familiar with this instance that we rarely realize its miraculous nature: this is the instance in which a certain body of matter becomes part of a living being.

Let's take a humble bacterium. Its physical constituents before and after it comes into being remain the same. But while the bacterium is in being ("alive") these constituents receive a new identity and unity that they did not have before it was "born" and will not have once it dies. In the brief interval of its life, the bacterium's "body parts" are (how else can we put it?) "body parts" — unified, individuated and energized by one center of action. As we have seen, when we say a physical being is living, we are saying that its physics, chemistry and biology have a "center," a moving force, a seat of power.

Leaving aside the question of origin, here we see that in the case of living beings their "matter" becomes the matter "of" a being — whether it be bacterium, plant, animal or human. The "of" part is what gives any living being's matter an identity and unity that the matter of Pluto and Mount Everest can never have. Although the matter in all these instances — that of Pluto, Mount Everest, a living being — is essentially the same from a physical standpoint, the "living matter" has a transphysical identity, unity and reality that makes it ontologically different from non-living matter.

("Ontology" concerns the fundamental structure of reality.) It is "life" that creates and constitutes this difference.

But, to repeat, by "life" we do not refer to an abstraction. We're talking about the life "of" a specific bacterium, plant, animal or human. Your body and blood, your flesh and blood have a distinct identity in being *yours*. And although, at a physical level, they are not essentially different from grains of sand, frozen icecaps or molten lava, they yet become a new and different reality simply by being part and parcel of your physical embodiment. Moreover, and this is important, you are present wherever your body and blood are present. When you talk of them as being your body and blood, you assume that they cannot exist separate or away from you. To give an unpleasant example, your finger ceases to be both "yours" and a finger if it is detached and crushed. It is no longer energized by your life and is therefore no longer yours.

If we take Jesus seriously, we affirm that the Divine Life becomes present in the matter that was once bread and wine. Now we are ready to examine what follows from the affirmation that the Eucharist is a vehicle of the Divine Life. In brief, *the introduction of the Divine Life changes the Eucharistic elements into the physical embodiment of the Divine Life*. And while at the fundamental physical level we are still dealing with the same protons, neutrons and electrons, they are now unified, individuated and energized by a new reality, the Divine Life.

But we have seen that there is no abstraction called "life." All "life" is the life of one specific agent or other. So "whose" life are we talking about when we talk about the Divine Life being present in the Eucharist? Those who recognize the Incarnation of God in Christ know that historically the Divine Life incarnated itself in matter in the person of Jesus of Nazareth (in him "dwells the whole fullness of the deity *bodily*" (Colossians 2:9)). Any subsequent instance of matter energized by the Divine Life would be one in which it is the Life of Jesus (God incarnate) that becomes present. And since the Eucharist is matter that has the Divine Life, the Life present in it is the Life of the incarnate Risen Lord.

If the Life of Jesus thus becomes present in the eucharistic elements then three things follow.

First, since the life of a human being in this world is embodied in flesh and blood and since the Risen Jesus is a human being, any material embodiment of his Life would be through his Body and Blood. Any matter in which his Life becomes present is transformed into his Body and Blood, his Flesh.

Secondly, in the case of human beings, there is no physical separation from the presence of the life of a person and the person itself. Thus I am present wherever my life is present. Likewise, Jesus is present wherever his Body and Blood are present. He is present physically and spiritually, body, soul and divinity.

Thirdly, while the protons, neutrons and electrons remain the same, they are now protons, neutrons and electrons "of" a living Being and therefore ontologically different in terms of identity, unity and efficacy.

Non-human animals are beings whose matter is governed and energized by their particular form of animal life. Human animals are beings whose matter is governed and energized by human life. The Eucharist is a new reality whose matter is governed and energized by the Divine Life of the incarnate Son of God. Non-human animals and human animals are different from each other (humans are rational animals because they have spiritual souls that are self-conscious and capable of conceptual thought). Likewise they are different from matter that is not energized by any kind of life. There is a difference, after all, between a human and a rock. But these differences pale before the distinction between the vehicles of created life and the Eucharist, the vehicle of the uncreated Life that brought all things (living and non-living) into being.

To recap, when the bread and the wine are consecrated, the subatomic particles that constitute it become the vehicles of the Life of the divine Person who became man, died for our sins and rose again. The question "How can bread and wine be the body and blood of Jesus?" rests on a misconception. At bottom, bread, wine, flesh, blood are all made up of the same sub-atomic particles, the same quantum fields. There is no unique set of protons, neutrons and electrons that make up bread or wine that is different from the set that makes up flesh and blood. The difference, if there is any, is at the ontological level, at the level of life and non-life.

The ontological difference between bread and wine, on the one hand, and body and blood, on the other, is the difference between matter and living matter. There is no fundamental physical difference between the subatomic constituents of bread and wine and those of your flesh and blood. The difference lies in the fact that the constituents in the latter instance are vehicles of your life. After the invocation of the Holy Spirit and the rite of consecration, the subatomic particles of the matter offered up to the Father now "embody" the Life of the incarnate Son of God.

To be sure, this "embodiment" does not involve a corresponding change in the observable physical properties of the Eucharistic elements. But, as modern science has shown us, "observable" should not be equated with "fundamental" or "essential." At the most fundamental level, there is no physical distinction between different aggregates of matter. The only kinds of fundamental distinctions are ontological in nature: between living and non-living beings and between different kinds of living beings. And this is precisely what we are talking about when we talk of the consecration of bread and wine into the Body and Blood of the living Christ.

Certainly, "observable" macro-level differences between various structures of matter become very important when matter serves as a vehicle of life. Let us call these different structures of matter "physical platforms." The physical "platforms" of microbes, plants, animals and humans had to be structured so as to be viable vehicles for their particular forms of life. Take, for instance, the intricate infrastructure of DNA and protein folding essential for all forms of biological life and the marvelously complex structure of the brain that is crucial for all human life. How this structuring of sub-atomic matter into various macroformations was done, how the match was made between platform and life-form is a fascinating question — as fascinating as the question of the origin of autonomous agency. But we are not concerned with this question here. Rather, we draw attention to this phenomenon of the structuring of physical platforms to see what light it throws on the external attributes of the Eucharist.

While bread and wine are not different from body and blood at the subatomic level, they are obviously different in terms of observable attributes at the macro-level. But, as we have seen, even these differences do not rule out the possibility of certain kinds of change taking place. Just as a blob of matter changes into your body and blood when it becomes a vehicle of your life at conception, bread and wine can change into Body and Blood when the matter that constitutes them becomes a platform of the Divine Life. *What is important here is that the specific platform whose matter is chosen for the Divine Life in Eucharistic consecration — bread and wine — is precisely the platform whose external properties are suitable for our ingestion as food and drink.* Because the platform does not change its external properties after consecration, it can be consumed by its intended recipients, namely human subjects. Just as all the other physical platforms of life were precisely structured for the appearance of the specific life-forms they support, so too was the platform of the Eucharist structured so as to support its end-objective, namely its consumption by humans. As we have seen, St. Thomas Aquinas pointed out that the sacrament of the Eucharist has the appearance of food and drink because it does for the soul what bread and wine do for the body.

Now while there is no change in their external properties, the Eucharistic elements do undergo an ontological change of being after consecration, a change driven by the coming of the Divine Life. This change, we have noted, has traditionally been called transubstantiation, a transformation of the underlying substance, and it is to this we shall turn again.

Transubstantiation in the light of the model of life

The traditional understanding of 'transubstantiation" is entirely consistent with the paradigm of life that is being presented here. In fact, transubstantiation is the most accurate and coherent description of this account of the supreme elevation of matter. This is because life as such can be thought of as a "substance" and the coming of life to what is previously lifeless is therefore a change of substance.

"Substance" has taken a lot of criticism in modern times (substance abuse of a different kind!). It is alleged that substance is an obsolete, Hellenistic idea. William Alston, a leading contemporary philosopher of language, has shown that most of these charges are simply false and that "substance" in the sense of ultimate substratum is a coherent and potent term.[6]

How does "substance" apply to "life"? In one of the only major modern studies of the ontological nature of life, Josef Seifert subjects this question to careful analysis. "Life is surely not accidental in this sense [Aristotle's sense of accident]. It characterizes the most elementary *what* and *how* something is, its substantial being and essence, and the activity and operation of an organism. Turning into a dead corpse, the organism changes its essence and loses its substantial identity. The corpse is no longer this animal or this human being: these no longer exist. Mere parts and external elements of the organism continue to exist after death that are not identical with the living whole that we call organism . . . The radical newness of life, of the *psyche*, the recognition of which we found to be the most important philosophical step in the discovery of the essence of life, shows that in addition to the living organism, life itself is a real entity. The principle of life, which in a sense is life or merges with it, is, at least in human persons, a substantial entity, a soul . . . The human soul is a simple substance that stands in itself in being."[7]

The application of these insightful passages to the present discussion is all but obvious. Recall the traditional affirmation of the Real Presence. "The whole Christ is truly present, body, blood, soul, and divinity, under the appearances of bread and wine — the glorified Christ who rose from the dead after dying for our sins."[8] Now consider a point made earlier: at consecration, lifeless matter becomes the vehicle of the Life of the Risen Lord thereby becoming his Body and Blood. We have seen that in humans "the principle of life is a substantial entity, a soul" and "soul" is "a simple substance that stands in itself in being." Since the "soul" of Christ becomes present at consecration ("And therefore in this sacrament the body indeed of Christ is present by the power of the sacrament, but His soul from real concomitance," wrote St. Thomas[9]), we see therefore that there is a change of substance. As to the matter that is the vehicle, there can be no change of "appearances" at the fundamental physical level, the sub-atomic realm, since all matter is made up of the same kinds of protons, neutrons and electrons. The only change that can and does take place is the introduction of the new Life-giving Substance that gives the previously existing protons, neutrons and electrons a new unity, identity and efficacy. What takes place, then, is a truly a change of substance, a transubstantiation.

All of the above ties into St. Thomas' explanation that transubstantiation is not an annihilation of the substance of bread and wine but its transformation. "The substance of the bread or wine, after the consecration, remains neither under the sacramental species, nor elsewhere; yet it does not follow that it is annihilated; for it is changed into the body of Christ; just as if the air, from which fire is generated, be not there or elsewhere, it does not follow that it is annihilated."[10]

Now what happens when you consume the Body and Blood of our Lord or when the Eucharistic elements decay or are destroyed by natural means of some kind? Since matter continues to be the same at the sub-atomic level, could it not be said that the Body and Blood will persist through all the changes undergone by their macro-level structures? Here the answer is as follows: what is transubstantiated is bread and wine, an aggregate that, in its external properties, can serve as food and drink. Jesus after all did not bestow the power to consecrate rocks and logs into his Body and Blood. Consequently, once the Eucharistic elements lose the properties of bread and wine, they are no longer carriers of the Divine Life. This, after all, is the case in other instances of the cessation of bodily functions. Once your heart stops beating and your kidneys and brain stop working, your life leaves what was previously your body. This is because your "physical platform" has to serve as a viable "platform" in order to sustain your life. The same applies to the Eucharist, the physical platform for the Divine Life. Said St. Thomas, "Since it does not seem reasonable to say that anything takes place miraculously in this sacrament, except in virtue of the consecration itself, which does not imply either creation or return of matter, it seems better to say that in the actual consecration it is miraculously bestowed on the dimensive quantity of the bread and wine to be the subject of subsequent forms."[11]

In saying that the Divine Life, the Soul and Divinity of Christ, become present in the Eucharistic elements so that they become the Body and Blood of Christ at consecration, we do not suggest that they are "living" in any sense of physical animation. St. Thomas points out, "The soul is the form of the body, giving it the whole order of perfect being, i.e., being, corporeal being, and animated being, and so on. Therefore the form of the bread is changed into the form of Christ's body, according as the latter gives corporeal being, but not according as it bestows animated being."[12] The life that is present is spiritual and not biological. It is personal, divine, eternal life.

Qualifications and caveats

The preceding model of life applied in describing the Eucharist has definite limitations. It is after all only a model for thinking about an enduring mystery and not a one-to-one description of the reality let alone an explanation. Any model of this mystery must acknowledge certain fundamental truths:

- The "This" in "This is my body" refers not to bread but to the new reality made present by the words themselves, a reality that retains the physical properties of bread.
- In the Eucharistic consecration the bread is not annihilated but neither does it "become" the Body of Christ since it is not "potentially" the Body or the matter from which the Body is made present: it is, however, the object on which the action of consecration is applied: but nothing of what was bread remains after the consecration: also the Body of Christ does not "begin" to exist after the consecration since here the matter is being "taken up" into a pre-existing reality.
- The Divine Life is present in the eucharistic "elements" after consecration but this Life does not have the characteristic of animation.

The attacks on Eucharistic doctrine launched over the last five hundred years and even some of the responses are focused entirely on the "how" rather than on what is actually relevant which is the "that." From the earliest days of the Discipline of the Secret, the Fathers and the liturgies as well as the faithful focused on the fact that the Eucharist is a vehicle of Divine Life. This indeed is where the focus should be. It is important to explore "how" it is the vehicle particularly in better proclaiming the "that." But what is all-important is the insight THAT the Eucharist is the vehicle of Divine Life. HOW it is the vehicle we will never fully understand. THAT it is so is what we know and hold and proclaim and live. Unfortunately from the time of Berengarius, the predecessor of the first critics, to the present day, the focus has been on the HOW with the subsequent loss of the THAT. In some communities that profess belief in the Eucharist, there is a tendency to downplay the THAT which is soon accompanied by a loss of the HOW. If you truly believe in the THAT, you will bear witness to it by your actions. The HOW is secondary. It is crucial to return to the THAT in liturgical celebrations and popular devotions if we wish to remain true to the primordial revelation.

The "life" model discussed here does not pretend to be a definitive account of the "how." The analogy used in the model is not intended to be the last word on how the Eucharistic transformation takes place. But anyone who wishes to retain and expound the "original" and definitive teaching of the community established by Jesus must hold that the Divine Life is present where IT was not. This is the Secret. Its preservation as originally handed down is the "Discipline of the Secret."

This is clear in the writings of the ancient Fathers as illustrated in these two passages from St. Cyril of Alexandria, the of the Council of Ephesus:

> God the Father gives life to all things through the Son, in the Holy Spirit. How, then was the human person, mastered on earth by death, to make his escape to incorruptibility? Necessarily, the flesh that was dying had to become a sharer in the life-giving power that comes from God. And the life- giving power of God the Father is the only-begotten Word. He sent him, then, as our savior and redeemer, and he became flesh ... So by eating the flesh of the Savior of us all, Christ, and by drinking his precious blood, we have life in ourselves and are formed to be one with him and remain in him, having him even within ourselves.[13]

> When the life-giving Word of God dwelt in human flesh, he changed it into that good thing which is distinctively his, namely, life; and by being wholly united to the flesh in a way beyond our comprehension, he gave it the life-giving power which he has by his very nature. Therefore, the body of Christ gives life to those who receive it. Its presence in mortal men expels death and drives away corruption because it contains within itself in his entirety the Word who totally abolishes corruption.[14]

If it is asked why an explication of the Eucharistic transformation is so complex and nuanced, we should note that the same might be asked of most scientific theories. To grasp the latter, we need to learn new concepts, adopt special vocabularies and digest new data. Any new insights into reality require the appropriate conceptual tools, relevant forms of reasoning and reliable starting points. The descent of the Divine Life is a fact of experience that must be taken on its own terms much as we address our experience of motion with applicable descriptions and laws.

No Dimensional Presence in the Eucharist

We have said earlier that God is present in the world in different ways. And we have just seen what is meant by saying that he is present in the Eucharist. A few questions pose themselves at this point. When the Eucharist is moved from place to place, is Jesus being moved as well since it is his Body? If two Hosts are present before us, are two Jesus' present as well? Does not consumption of the Host cause actual physical injury to Christ if it is indeed his Body?

In response it is said that the presence of Christ in the Eucharist is "sacramental" and therefore such questions are meaningless. But what does it mean to say the presence is sacramental and how does it address the questions without diminishing the reality of the divine Presence?

The short answer is that Jesus is not present dimensionally in the Eucharist. "The dimensions of the bread or wine are not changed into the dimensions of the body of Christ," wrote St. Thomas Aquinas, "but substance into substance. And so the substance of Christ's body or blood is under this sacrament by the power of the sacrament, but not the dimensions of Christ's body or blood."[15] "Christ's body is not in this sacrament in the same way as a body is in a place, which by its dimensions is commensurate with the place; but in a special manner which is proper to this sacrament. Hence we say that Christ's body is upon many altars, not as in different places, but "sacramentally": and thereby we do not understand that Christ is there only as in a sign, although a sacrament is a kind of sign; but that Christ's body is here after a fashion proper to this sacrament, as stated above."[16]

The manner of Jesus' presence in his Eucharistic Body, then, is unique. It is true that God — and this means the Trinity — is present everywhere. But God Incarnate, Jesus in his human nature, is today present only in Heaven and in the Eucharist. At consecration, Jesus does not come down from Heaven to the Host but the Host rises to him. The earthly rises to the heavenly. To participate in the Mass is to participate in the offering of Jesus to the Father which continues in Heaven *("he lives forever to make intercession for them."* Hebrews 7:25) and to receive the Bread from Heaven. (Heaven, incidentally, is not a place "above" the sky but a radically different state of being. We will see more on this in the next chapter).

Thus Christ's Body is not "locally" present. St. Thomas again, "Christ is not moved locally of Himself, but only accidentally, because Christ is not in this sacrament as in a place, as stated above. But what is not in a place, is not moved of itself locally, but only according to the motion of the subject in which it is."[17]

We have spoken of the Eucharist as the vehicle of Divine Life because it is the Flesh and Blood of the Second Person of the Trinity in his human nature. Every encounter with the Divine Life that is in the Eucharist is simultaneously an encounter with him who possesses that Life, the Risen Christ. It is the presence of Jesus in us in his Divine Life that led the Apostle Paul to write, "Yet I live, no longer I, but Christ lives in me." (Galatians 2:20).

What brings about the transformation we call transubstantiation? It is the action of Christ for as St. John Chrysostom declares, "It is not man that causes the things offered to become the Body and Blood of Christ, but he who was crucified for us, Christ himself. The priest, in the role of Christ, pronounces these words, but their power and grace are God's. This is my body, he says. This word transforms the things offered."[18] Likewise St. Ambrose says, "Be convinced that this is not what nature has formed, but what the blessing has consecrated. The power of the blessing prevails over that of nature, because by the blessing nature itself is changed. . . . Could not Christ's word, which can make from nothing what did not exist, change existing things into what they were not before? It is no less a feat to give things their original nature than to change their nature."[19]

What Does it Mean to Receive Divine Life

The Eucharist should be understood in the context of the underlying revelation of divinization which is the divine invitation for human beings to participate in the Life of God. In fact, the transformation of the eucharistic elements into physical vehicles for the Life of God has a parallel in divinization. When we receive baptism and the other sacraments, in particular the Eucharist, we directly receive the Divine Life. This is what it means to say we are divinized. But there is a difference between divinization and the Eucharist. After consecration, the whole reality of the Eucharist is transformed so that it becomes entirely and only a vehicle of the Divine Life albeit clothed in creaturely appearances. Divinized human beings, however, retain their human life and identity.

If someone were to ask what there is that is different about a person before and after being divinized, the answer, in a word, is the Life that is now present in him or her. The divinized person lives with the infinite Energy of the Divine Life. But this Energy can be experienced only to the extent that the person removes obstacles to the operation of the Divine Life in the soul.

Can you see this Life, it may be asked. The answer is "No" for the simple reason that neither human life nor Divine Life is something you can see. Human life, of course, manifests itself through various actions such as locomotion, speech and the like. The Divine Life, the Life that creates and transforms, manifests itself in its action on the soul.

Even in our everyday experience, the huge amounts of energy latent in what appears to be the most inert units of matter is hidden to view. The equivalence of mass and energy expressed in Albert Einstein's formula $e=mc^2$ tells us that the energy contained in any material object at rest is derived by multiplying its mass m by c^2 the square of the speed of light (186,000 miles per second) – or, as Einstein put it, "The energy that belongs to the mass m is equal to this mass, multiplied by the square of the enormous speed of light – which is to say, a vast amount of energy for every unit of mass." The fact that something is motionless says nothing about whether or not it is actually exploding with energy.

Einstein himself noted this paradox: "But if every gram of material contains this tremendous energy, why did it go so long unnoticed? The answer is simple enough: so long as none of the energy is given off externally, it cannot be observed. It is as though a man who is fabulously rich should never spend or give away a cent; no one could tell how rich he was."[20] The equivalence of mass and energy was confirmed most dramatically -- and tragically -- by the atom bomb. Just 20 pounds of plutonium can blow up an entire city with a destructive force of 70 million pounds of TNT. The relevance of the mass-energy equation to the doctrine of the divinization is simply this: the external characteristics of a thing rarely reflect its inherent power.

Some might ask: but what does it mean to "receive" the Divine Life? Is the Divine Life a kind of liquid that can be poured into the soul?

We have seen earlier that there is a hierarchy of life. The kind of acts that we are able to perform tells us what kind of life we have, what kind of being we are. If we can think and walk and talk and make free choices, then we are beings with human nature. To receive the Divine Life and thus to be divinized (assuming no barrier), is to perform acts that go beyond human nature, to possess a kind of life that allows you to live without end in union with God.

By receiving the Divine Life, you are elevated as a person. You receives new powers and become capable of new acts. You can think in a way that was not possible with deepening discernment and an ongoing cascade of insights.. You are purified, you receive a new energy of spirit and body. Above all, you receive the power to love without limit.

For life on earth to continue we need physical energy which we receive from the kinds of physical food we consume that are then converted into energy. For the Divine Life to continue in our being, we need to first NOT perform any act that kills it (just as physical life can be jeopardized by reckless acts). Secondly we need to nurture and nourish it: hence the need to continually receive the Divine Life in the Eucharist.

In this context, it may be asked why the Divine Life is being transmitted to us through a physical vehicle. Here the answer is simple if not obvious.

The Eucharist has to be physical and spiritual because the human person is physical and spiritual. The Hebraic revelation remained true to a vision of human beings as intrinsically ensouled and embodied. We are not pure spirits trapped in a physical container as Plato assumed. The human person is a union of spirit and matter. This is why the Eucharist (like all the sacraments) is both physical and spiritual. It is true to what we are.

One final point: the transmission of Divine Life through the Eucharist is not an impersonal transaction. There is no "life" in general only living beings. The same is true with God. When the Divine Life is present, God is present, drawing us into his triune Love. And to receive the Eucharist is to receive the Divine Love. In no other case do we hear of one form of life "entering" another. It is only possible with the Divine Life which is the Source and Sustainer of all Life.

THE KILLER APP OF THE DIVINE LIFE SOCIAL NETWORK IS LIFE ∞.0 IN THE DIVINE BIOSPHERE

Chapter 8

The Eucharist is Eternal Life Here and Now, the Life of Heaven

We spoke in the beginning of the astounding claim that humanity has been called to share in the Life of God. We have seen how this call manifested itself in the depths of the human psyche from the dawn of recorded history. In the fullness of time, the invitation was delivered to the human race by God himself who took on a human nature so that we might share in the divine nature. The invitation sits in the "Inbox" of our souls. The question now is whether we want to reply to it by joining the Divine Life Social Network. And since we have reviewed the features and functions of the social network, it is perhaps time to consider its benefits.

Like any social network, its primary benefits are the ability to communicate, share and create our own timeline. We are able to Communicate with God himself – face to face. We will be able to Share in the very Life of God. And we will create a Timeline that extends to eternity, an eternity of ecstasy.

All three are directly connected. The Life of God in fact is the Life of the divine Biosphere, what we call Heaven. Of course many moderners view Heaven as an archaic superstition not fit for discussion in educated company (although Hell retains value as an expletive). But one key element of the Secret is that the divine Biosphere begins here and now. Divinization, in fact, is the entry point to Heaven. Given the importance of Heaven for human destiny, we should address common misconceptions and present what can be known.

To this end we will review the relevant issues:

- ❖ Beliefs of the Unbelievers
- ❖ Heaven as the Divine Biosphere
- ❖ The Eucharist and the Divine Force-Field
- ❖ The Eucharist as Energy-Source and Soul-Food
- ❖ The Blessed Virgin, Spouse of the Holy Spirit and Model of Divinization
- ❖ Sin, Holiness, Love and the Holy Mass

Beliefs of the Unbelievers

The modern distaste for Heaven can be partially traced to an overall loss of any sense of realities that lie beyond sensory perception. Paradoxically, the drumbeaters for science, who dismiss Heaven with adolescent levity, ardently promote ideas of numerous unseen dimensions and a multitude of universes. We are assured that these exist despite the lack of any evidence for their existence. We are admonished against asking for evidence for the missing dimensions and universes. In lowered tones we are told that it will never be possible to scientifically verify their existence because they lie outside our space-time framework. So why believe in them or assert their existence so confidently given that a claim is scientific only if it is capable of being scientifically tested? Well, the equations are so elegant, the theories so tantalizing, the old rules do not apply. Apparently there is no problem with blind faith as long as the object of belief is dressed up in the right vocabulary.

In addressing the skeptics let us say this:

The first and most stunning mystery is that we are here and that anything is here. We can be here only if SOMETHING always was here. But how could that Something ALWAYS be, exist ALWAYS? We cannot know but we do know if that Something did not exist ALWAYS, nothing would exist. We face the unthinkable, unimaginable fact that God always

IS – there is no beginning, no end in God. But how is this possible? The answer is that we can have no idea HOW but we do know THAT it is the case – else there is no explanation for anything else existing. You do know that things exist. You want to know how anything at all exists – ever. You cannot buy the idea that things just happened to exist without rhyme or reason all the "time". But what is the logic that made it all happen? The only way this question can be addressed is by recognizing the fact that there would have to exist some supremely rational and utterly perfect being that always existed and also brought all other things into existence (from its own power and freewill). Either there is such a being or there should be nothing at all around. Having said this, you are no closer to grasping how it is possible that this Something ALWAYS existed without beginning or end – this is just a hard fact that you have to accept if you want to make sense of the world.

But what was that Something doing in its ALWAYS existence? This is where the Light of the Holy Trinity pierces the darkness. We know that loving and total self-giving is the Ultimate Reality: THIS is what always was and is and will be. The giving of one infinite Person to the Other, the loving of the Three that makes Them One, this is the ultimate truth about things, this is Reality. It is only in seeing this that everything else makes sense, most particularly the life of Jesus of Nazareth, the Son of God made man, the Redeemer who gave up his Life to save us from our sins. And it is only in seeing this endless explosion of Love that the Eucharistic celebration makes sense for in the Holy Mass we participate in the eternal offering up of the Son to the Father in the unity of the Holy Spirit.

The stunning fact that there is infinite self-giving Love at the heart of reality changes everything, all our assumptions, expectations and goals. The Why of everything can be understood once we understand the reality of the Holy Trinity. Why is anything here and why is it the way it is and how is it supposed to be? Because Love brought it into being so as to create a divine Biosphere of endless joy. Why then is there pain and suffering, savagery and catastrophe? Why does an all-loving God allow evil? Because love by its nature is built on freedom and freedom by its nature makes it possible to choose lesser goods over the greatest Good. A choice that rejects the divine Love results in pain and suffering because it is a rejection of what we were built for. But it is sadly a choice continuously made by human persons and pure spirits with all the attendant tragic consequences.

But so great is the divine Love and so precious is every human person that God became man and died to save us from the consequences of our choices while sharing in our suffering. It is this Love that manifests itself in every celebration of the Eucharist empowering us anew to choose what is best for us, to create here and now a Biosphere of divine Love that reaches into eternity.

What about those who say no to God and his Biosphere? Scientists talk about parallel universes. While there is no scientific evidence possible for this speculative idea and therefore no reason to believe in the existence of such universes, it is a useful model in contemplating the fabric of ultimate reality – a fabric that goes beyond all of physical reality and is only known to us because it was revealed by the Author of reality. The alternative to the divine Biosphere is a Necrosphere of undying death. Those who choose their selves over God will be given what they choose: they will live forever just with their own selves and with all who have similarly rejected the divine Love. There are two parallel immaterial universes that extend into eternity – the divine Biosphere and the diabolic Necrosphere. Each human person as also each pure spirit (an angel) chooses its own destiny, its own preferred universe, its own ultimate social network.

Our concern here is with the destiny for which we have been created and to which we have been invited by the God who is Love, namely the divine Biosphere. It is this that we call Heaven.

Heaven as the Divine Biosphere

It is after we have discovered God that we encounter Heaven. Heaven is not a topic to be discussed with the mystically challenged. Its contemplation demands a minimal level of discernment that goes beyond quantitative measurement and numerical calculations. It requires comprehension of the stupendous fact that the supraphysical reality we call spirit does not occupy space. God is infinite Spirit. The human person is a union of spirit and matter. It is easy to see why spirit does not occupy space. If we ask where the "I" that is me or you is located we cannot point to any part of our bodies. The Creator of the "I" and of all else likewise does not occupy space – and yet He is the Creator of space, time and matter. He created them out of nothingness. Once we realize that "spirit" by its very nature is immeasurably superior to matter and to any physical dimension (and by dimension we mean a direction in which physical entities can move) we realize the mystery and power of the divine Life.

So where is Heaven? With regard to "where" we have to make it clear that it is in no respect physical in the sense we currently experience the physical. Then again, neither God nor the angels are physical: they are wholly spiritual. They are present "where" they act. To enter Heaven is not to enter a new material dimension. Rather we experience a new state of being that infinitely surpasses all that we have encountered in our current state. Of course, through the revelation of God in Jesus we learn that, in the hereafter, human beings will be fully reconstituted with a resurrected body (and only in this way can we be truly human). But this "body" will be entirely different in capability from our present bodies. Moreover, humans will commune with angels and God who are bodiless by nature. The question with regard to Heaven should be "what" rather than "where." There is only so far you can go with an imagination formed entirely by our three-dimensional world.

Speculation about Heaven in purely human terms is pointless because, by its very nature, the immediate knowledge and love of God is something the human person cannot enjoy in this life and hence cannot describe or grasp. But we know that Heaven is a union with the Creator of this immense universe, with the Author of all the love, goodness, and joy around us, with the One in whom all these are found in perfection. We know that such union cannot but bring him the highest possible satisfaction and happiness. All physical and spiritual pleasures in this world derive from God who is the Source of all joy. They are only hints and harbingers of the final and direct union with him at "Whose right hand there are pleasures forevermore." There is an almost terrifying ecstasy, a fearful joy, in the thought of union with the Creator, the Inventor, of galaxies and pine trees, sunsets and smiles, babies and giraffes, angels and the Alps.

But while saying that Heaven is indescribable in terrestrial terms, there is continuity between life on earth and in Heaven, a continuity that is especially apparent in divinization and the Eucharist.

The Eucharist and the Divine Force-Field

One way of talking about divinization, Heaven and the here-and-now is to use yet another analogy from science, this time of fields.

Modern physics has shown that all physical entities are basically energy fields. A field is something that has energy and occupies space. All the matter, all the physical forces in the world are ultimately fields and so they are not different in kind. A matter field simply has a higher concentration of energy than a "matter-less" field. Particles like electrons and photons are produced by ripples of energy in a field: they are forms of concentrated energy.

The spiritual world is irreducibly different from the world of matter and energy because spirit does not occupy space. But we can analogically talk of a divine force-field that is concentrated at certain points to form particles. Now these points are persons and the particles are persons who become divinized when the Spirit of God "comes upon" them. The analogy is limited because these persons do not become part of God. They are not the divine force-field. They are beings distinct from it. The divine force-field, of course, has infinite Energy and brought all things, physical and spiritual, into being. Nevertheless, those who are divinized take on characteristics of the force-field and to that extent they become manifestations of the effect of the field. When the Spirit of God touches a soul it is "filled with the Spirit". It acts with the Power of the Spirit and manifests the Presence of the Spirit. The Spirit is divine, the Spirit-filled person is divinized.

When we talk of the divine Biosphere we refer to the manifestation of the divine force-field. This reaches its culmination in the direct unmediated union with God that is Heaven. But it is also operative here and now. The greatest channel of the force-field in this world is the Eucharist and it is in adoring and receiving the Eucharist that we have the opportunity to "taste and see that the Lord is good."

The Eucharist is Jesus here and now with us. Hence we worship the Blessed Sacrament. When we pray before the Tabernacle, we are speaking to Jesus. The more we pray to the Eucharistic Jesus, the more we become aware that we are really and truly in the presence of the same Jesus who delivered the Sermon on the Mount and was crucified on Calvary. It is here before him that we find healing for the loneliness of the human heart. All our experiences, memories, intuitions, wounds, yearnings are sanctified, elevated, divinized. And in coming before the Eucharist and in participating in the Holy Mass we meet Jesus. But it is not simply a question of us meeting Jesus but of Jesus meeting us. Moreover, our conversation with the Eucharistic Jesus is consummated in Eucharistic communion whereby we receive his life-giving Flesh and Blood. We receive the divine Life so that "yet I live, no longer I, but Christ lives in me." (Galatians 2:20).

When we participate in the liturgy of the Eucharist, all our needs and weaknesses and we ourselves are taken up into the Holy Sacrifice. We are in the presence of the wholly Other. In this timeless event we are united with all our loved ones living and dead, with all the saints and angels and most especially the Holy Family. When the Mass is celebrated before us, we have to realize that WE are offering the Sacrifice as well. It is a mystical event that unites all who participate – those in Heaven, those departed souls who are being purified in preparation for Heaven and whom we assist by remembering in the sacred celebration, and we who are physically present. If the ancient pagan sacrifices were deadly serious occasions in which the whole community came together bedecked in solemn splendor to express the desires of their hearts, it behooves us who participate in the supreme and living Sacrifice to act no less solemnly. In the Mass, the divine Other becomes present, physically and spiritually, and imparts to us the divine Life.

To us who drown in evil, savagery, pain, suffering and the separation from all of our loved ones that is death, there is a single ray of sunshine in the darkness: the rumor of One who rose again, who is himself divine Life and who offers this very life to all who follow him and his teaching. If this rumor is true, everything is transformed: our lives are connected to a hereafter that begins here-and-now and all our choices and acts take on eternal meaning and significance. If it is true, then we who are always sinning, who are always being rushed to the ER with terminal wounds, receive what St. Ignatius of Antioch called "the medicine of immortality, the antidote to prevent us from dying", a medicine that expiates, purifies, sanctifies, elevates, strengthens, a medicine that revives us from the coma induced by toxins from without and within. If it is true, then it is of the utmost importance that this message be preserved in the midst of the cacophony of constant inconstancy that is the world: of myriad teachings, ideologies, fashions; pressures to conform, change, dilute, reconstruct and "modernize."

For the first followers of Jesus, the celebration of the Eucharist was the central event of their lives and of world history thereafter. Hence everything else revolved around it. Hence they preserved it for posterity with the Discipline of the Secret, guarding and transmitting the sacred treasure in all its fullness. In the teeth of opposition from individuals and institutions, the Guardian of the Secret, "the pillar and foundation of truth," has remained faithful from the beginning to the present day to her mission of proclaiming and disseminating the Divine Genome.

The Eucharist as Energy-Source and Soul-Food

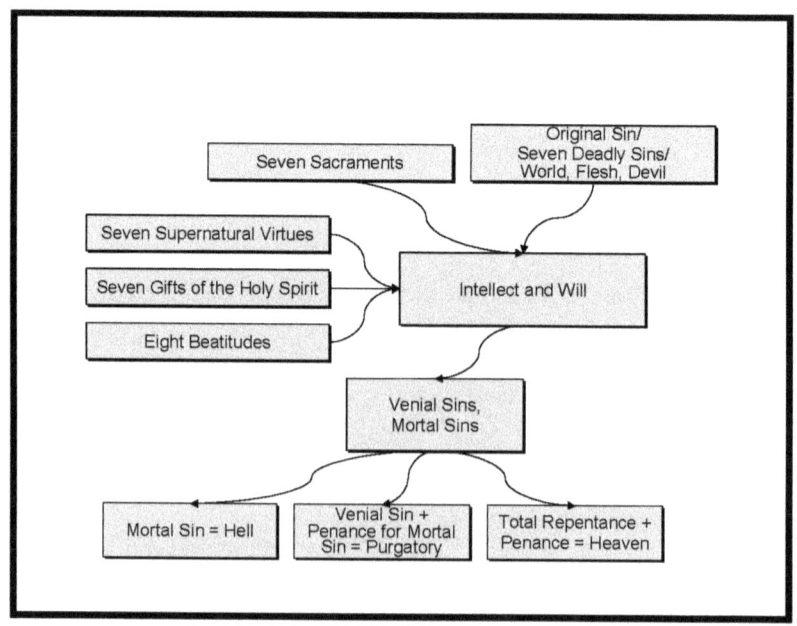

To recap, the Divine Genome as manifested in the Eucharist – the divine Life energizing the eucharistic elements, the resultant conversion of these elements into the (sacramentally present) physical being of God incarnate – makes perfect sense of the religious heritage of humanity, the inspired texts of the Hebrew Bible and the New Testament and the teachings of the Councils and the Fathers. The code-words of Jesus are unutterably meaningful in the present setting:

> *"Take and eat; this is my body."*
>
> *"This is my blood of the covenant, which will be shed for many."*
>
> *"Whoever eats this bread will live forever; and the bread that I will give is my flesh for the life of the world."*
>
> *"Whoever eats my flesh and drinks my blood has eternal life, and I will raise him on the last day."*
>
> *"Whoever eats my flesh and drinks my blood remains in me and I in him."*

At one and the same time they mask and manifest the mystery of Heaven coming down to Earth, the Transcendent meeting the Immanent. We see why St. Paul warns,

> For anyone who eats and drinks without discerning the body, eats and drinks judgment on himself. That is why many among you are ill and infirm, and a considerable number are dying." (I Corinthians 11:29-30).

If bread and wine were simply symbols, they could not *in themselves* be the cause of such drastic consequences. For *"The cup of blessing that we bless, is it not a participation in the blood of Christ? The bread that we break, is it not a participation in the body of Christ?"* (I Corinthians 10:16).

We return one final time to the question of what happens when we receive the Eucharist. We saw that the presence of the divine Life in the eucharistic elements not simply individuates and unifies them but also gives them a new efficacy. But what does this mean in concrete terms? If the Eucharist is a carrier of the divine Life, how does this help its recipients?

Consider food in general. Food is the source of our energy. We receive energy from the carbohydrates and proteins contained in our foods. These foods are, in general, derived from other living beings be they plant or animal. We receive our physical energy from them. Their "flesh and blood" become part of our body and blood.

Consider now the Food from Heaven, the Body and Blood of God incarnate. As a carrier of the divine Life, it imparts its Life and associated spiritual Energy to its recipients. As the Fathers recognized, it divinizes the soul of the recipient who is rightly inclined. Just as Jesus' Body and Blood pass into our body and blood, his Soul and Divinity enter our souls and natures transforming them. "The cup of blessing that we bless, is it not a participation in the blood of Christ? The bread that we break, is it not a participation in the body of Christ? Because the loaf of bread is one, we, though many, are one body, for we all partake of the one loaf." (1 Corinthians 10:16-17).

What precisely are the characteristics or properties of the Divine Life that are transmitted in and through the Eucharist? How is the Divine Life actualized? Clearly, as we have seen, we are not dealing with the attributes of animation (motion, for instance) that we normally associate with biological life. Then again, higher forms of life are characterized by higher-level activities that are hidden and yet immeasurably more profound: conceptual thought and unconditional love above all. And this indeed applies to the Divine Life. It is an Energy that acts at the level of intellect and will elevating the two powers of our souls, knowing and loving. "Christ's body is not changed into man's body, but nourishes his soul," wrote St. Thomas.[1]

The Eucharist divinizes us. To be divinized is to live with the Life of God and to know and love with the Power of God. We "share in the divine nature" (2 Peter 1:4) because "whoever is joined to the Lord becomes one spirit with him." (I Corinthians 6:17). To be divinized is to undergo a radical and total transformation in and through God by being filled with the Holy Spirit. Among the "properties" associated with the divinized life are the seven Gifts of the Spirit and the supernatural virtues.

The gifts of the Spirit are gifts that we are free to accept or reject. The gifts protect and perfect the supernatural virtues. The seven gifts of the Spirit divinize the two human powers that image God: intellect and will. Wisdom, understanding, counsel and knowledge are the gifts that transform the intellect while fortitude, piety, and fear of the Lord crown the will and the emotions. The direct cause of these gifts is the Holy Spirit. A weakened will and darkened intellect are the common lot of humanity and this includes those who possess the divine Life and the supernatural virtues. Some divine impetus is required at all times to protect us against ourselves and this is where the gifts come in. It is impossible to exaggerate the power of the gifts of the Spirit. Imagine if you will that you were suddenly granted the genius of an Einstein and the fortitude of an Alexander, the wisdom of a Solomon and the courage of a David. In point of fact, the divinizing gifts actually elevate our thinking and acting infinitely beyond the capabilities of these human prodigies.

The supernatural virtues are new "habits" and "powers" of the soul inherited by us when we receive the Life of God. They are habits of doing good. They are instantaneous, not acquired over time but given by God. These virtues, which are laid out in Scripture, are of two kinds: theological virtues (faith, hope and charity), those directly oriented to God, i.e., those that have God as their immediate object; and cardinal virtues (prudence, justice, fortitude and temperance), those that help orient us to God. The supernatural virtues represent the true path to happiness. Each virtue, as a great scholar has put it, constitutes a particular dimension of happiness: Faith – happiness of the mind; Hope – happiness of the heart; Charity – the happiness of God; Prudence – happiness in action; Justice – happiness in society; Fortitude – happiness in heroism; Temperance – happiness in self-control. Although infused in us as part of the divine Life, the supernatural virtues can be retained and built up only by our continuing perseverance and recourse to the sacraments.

	Intellect	Will
Supernatural Theological Virtues		
	Faith	
		Hope
		Charity
Supernatural Cardinal Virtues		
	Prudence	
		Justice
		Fortitude
		Temperance
Divinizing Gifts of the Holy Spirit		
	Wisdom	
	Understanding	
	Knowledge	
	Counsel	
		Fortitude
		Piety
		Fear of the Lord
Beatitudes		
	Peacemakers	
	Pure of heart	
	Mourners	
	Merciful	
		Meek
		Hunger after justice
		Persecuted
		Poor in Spirit

The indwelling of the Spirit that comes through the sacraments, supernatural virtues and divinizing gifts bears fruit in our attitudes, acts, outlook, habits, emotions, moods and our being as a whole. The Divine

Life transforms us from root to fruit. St. Paul calls these changes the fruit of the Spirit; they are the "first fruits" of glory. Paul mentions several fruits (nine in some translations, twelve in others) but clearly his list is not meant to be exhaustive. The fruit of the Spirit, says the Apostle, "is love, joy, peace, patience, kindness, generosity, faithfulness, gentleness, self-control." (Galatians 5:22-3). The fruits belong to three domains: yourself (love, joy, peace); neighbor (patience, kindness, generosity, gentleness, faithfulness) and external actions (self-control).

St. Paul contrasts these fruits of the Spirit to the works of the flesh. "The works of the flesh are obvious: immorality, impurity, licentiousness, idolatry, sorcery, hatreds, rivalry, jealousy, outbursts of fury, acts of selfishness, dissensions, factions, occasions of envy, drinking bouts, orgies, and the like." (Galatians 5:19-21). Those who do such things, he warns, "will not inherit the kingdom of God." (21). Only the divine Life that is the Spirit can rescue us from the irresistible lure of the flesh. "Live by the Spirit and you will certainly not gratify the desire of the flesh. For the flesh has desires against the Spirit and the Spirit against the flesh; these are opposed to each other, so that you may not do what you want." (16-18). Furthermore, "those who belong to Christ have crucified their flesh with its passions and desires." The endgame is this: "A person will reap only what he sows, because the one who sows for his flesh will reap corruption from the flesh, but the one who sows for the spirit will reap eternal life from the spirit." (6:7-8).

Jesus shows us just how important are the fruits in the final reckoning: "Every good tree bears good fruit, and a rotten tree bears bad fruit. A good tree cannot bear bad fruit, nor can a rotten tree bear good fruit. Every tree that does not bear good fruit will be cut down and thrown into the fire. So by their fruits you will know them." (Matthew 7:17-20). In the parable of the fig tree, he points to the supernatural assistance that is given to all but can still be resisted: "I shall cultivate the ground around it and fertilize it; it may bear fruit in the future. If not you can cut it down." (Luke 13: 8-9).

There are degrees of divinization just as there are degrees of physical health: some people are healthier than others. Often enough our physical health is determined by our own intentions and acts in the areas of diet, exercise and preventive maintenance. So it is with divinization. The full "effect" of the sacraments depends on a diet of prayer, exercise of the virtues and the preventive maintenance of mortification. Imagine, if you will, that you take some kind of energy therapy that requires both physical and psychological preparation to be effective. The therapy works through a combination of mental acts, dieting practices, exercise regimens and specific nutrients that enable the right absorption, bio-availability and epigenetic action. Divinization likewise requires us to be in touch with God with our minds and hearts, to desire the infusion of Life that comes with the sacraments, to purify ourselves through the examination of conscience and the sacrament of reconciliation, to avoid all that leads us away from God. In receiving the Eucharist, we become tabernacles of God and God cannot remain in the same "place" as impurity, evil or lack of love.

The Blessed Virgin, Spouse of the Holy Spirit and Model of Divinization

In speaking of degrees of divinization, we note that the highest of all divinized human persons is the Mother of Jesus. Her "Yes" to the Father made possible the Incarnation of the Son of God. She became the Spouse of the Holy Spirit and Mother of the Son.

The Holy Spirit's "overshadowing" of Mary at the Annunciation is a mirror image of the Exodus passage describing Yahweh's coming into the tabernacle. "The Holy Spirit will come upon you and the power of the Most High will cover you with its shadow." (Luke 1:35). "The cloud covered the Tent of Meeting and the glory of Yahweh filled the tabernacle." (Exodus 40:34). Biblical scholars have argued that other verses concerning Mary in the Gospels of Luke and John parallel passages about the Ark of the Covenant in the Old Testament. Moreover, Mary's prayers help bring about the greatest outpouring of the Spirit in history, Pentecost. Three direct interventions of the Holy Spirit in the Gospels involve Mary: the Annunciation when the Spirit overshadows her, the Visitation when the Holy Spirit inspires Elizabeth, the Presentation when Simeon too is inspired by the Spirit. The Rosary in its essence is specifically a prayer directly inspired by the Holy Spirit: "And Elizabeth was filled with the Holy Spirit. She gave a loud cry and said, 'Of all women you are the most blessed, and blessed is the fruit of your womb." (Luke 1:42).

Not surprisingly Mary has been the human person most closely identified with the Holy Spirit throughout Christian history. The Second Council of Nicaea, formally addressed Mary by her ancient title *Panagia* meaning "all-holy"; the masculine form of this Greek word is *Panagion*, the title of the Holy Spirit. In other words, this Council, accepted by all Christians, called Mary and the Holy Spirit by the same name! This same Council also decreed in so many words what all the other Councils assumed: she is "higher than all creatures visible and invisible" and all Christians must "implore with a sincere faith, her intercession, given her powerful access to our God born of her."

Accounts of the appearances of the Virgin Mary are found in all the great cultures of the world. Tangible miraculous objects from these apparitions – such as the tilma/cloak of Guadalupe with the miraculous image of the Virgin and the healing spring of Lourdes – continue to exert immense power to this day. Moreover the messages associated with these hundreds of cross-cultural appearances are so remarkably similar as to suggest a single script-writer. All the apparitions of the Virgin are intimately related to the divinizing mission of the Spirit. In her apparitions, the concern of the Virgin is conversion from sin, growth in holiness and the reception of the Holy Eucharist. In her apparition to St. Catherine Laboure (famous for the Miraculous Medal), she said: "Come to the front of the altar. There graces will be shed upon all, great and small who ask for them. Especially will graces be shed upon those who ask for them." As was apparent from the earliest days of the Christian faith, the Virgin Mary, well described by the poet William Wordsworth as "our tainted nature's solitary boast," is a maternal model and guide on the journey of divinization.

Sin, Holiness, Love and the Holy Mass

Returning to divinization, we see that its ultimate goal, and thus of the Eucharist, is to transform us into vessels of holiness and love: this is the purpose of creation, incarnation and redemption: this is what God is. If we ask what is most important about the Eucharist in our daily lives, the answer lies in the actual words of the divine liturgy. Consider the words of institution in the Latin rite Mass:

He took bread and, giving thanks, broke it, and gave it to his disciples, saying: TAKE THIS, ALL OF YOU, AND EAT OF IT, FOR THIS IS MY BODY, **WHICH WILL BE GIVEN UP FOR YOU**. …

He took the chalice and, once more giving thanks, he gave it to his disciples, saying:

TAKE THIS, ALL OF YOU, AND DRINK FROM IT, FOR THIS IS THE CHALICE OF MY BLOOD, THE BLOOD OF THE NEW AND ETERNAL COVENANT, **WHICH WILL BE POURED OUT FOR YOU** AND FOR MANY FOR THE FORGIVENESS OF SINS.

After the consecration we repeat: "Lamb of God, **you take away the sins of the world**, have mercy on us." And then the priest prays, "Free me by this, your most holy Body and Blood, **from all my sins and from every evil**; keep me always faithful to your commandments, and never let me be parted from you." Then raising the sacred Host, he proclaims: "Behold the Lamb of God, **behold him who takes away the sins of the world**." In response the faithful say, "Lord, I am not worthy that you should enter under my roof, but only say the word and **my soul shall be healed**."

Only when we realize our own wretchedness, our desperately evil state, can we fully appreciate what is being offered at each and every Mass. We are being freed of a burden that constantly drags us down, healed of a wound that grows worse by the day, cured of a cancer that is terminal. We are being liberated from the slavery of sin and its attendant fear and sorrow. At each Mass we make our own the prayer handed down in the Divine Mercy revelation: "Eternal Father, I offer you the Body and Blood, Soul and Divinity, of Your Dearly Beloved Son, Our Lord, Jesus Christ, **in atonement for our sins** and those of the whole world." Jesus came to us precisely because we are sick: "Those who are well do not need a physician, but the sick do. … I did not come to call the righteous but sinners." (Matthew 9:11-13). And the treatment he administers is the "medicine of immortality."

Heaven on Earth!

But our goal is not simply to avoid sin. Our primary focus is on loving God and his creatures without limit or condition. To love God means to keep his law of love and holiness. Love is an act of the will and to love God is to align our wills to the divine Will. We are empowered to align our wills with God's will through reception of the Eucharist. After praying that "thy will be done on earth as it is in Heaven," we ask the Father to "give us this day our daily bread," the bread of Life. We need this divine sustenance because we are called to the perfection of God which is a perfection of love and holiness.

"Love your enemies, and pray for those who persecute you, that you may be children of your heavenly Father ….Be perfect, just as your heavenly Father is perfect." (Matthew 5:44-45,48). "Beloved, let us love one another, because love is of God; everyone who loves is begotten by God and knows God. Whoever is without love does not know God, for God is love. In this way the love of God was revealed to us: God sent his only Son into the world so that we might have life through him. In this is love: not that we have loved God, but that he loved us and sent his Son as expiation for our sins. Beloved, if God so loved us, we also must love one another. No one has ever seen God. Yet, if we love one another, God remains in us, and his love is brought to perfection in us. This is how we know that we remain in him and he in us, that he has given us of his Spirit." (1 John 4:7-13).. "We love because he first loved us. If anyone says, 'I love God,' but hates his brother, he is a liar; for whoever does not love a brother whom he has seen cannot love God whom he has not seen." (1 John 4:19-20). "The way we may be sure that we know him is to keep his commandments. Whoever says, 'I know him,' but does not keep his commandments is a liar, and the truth is not in him. But whoever keeps his word, the love of God is truly perfected in him. This is the way we may know that we are in union with him." (1 John 2:3-5). "For our sake he made him to be sin who did not know sin, so that we might become the righteousness of God in him." (2 Corinthians 5:21). "Strive for … that holiness without which no one will see the Lord." (Hebrews 12:14). "God disciplines us … in order that we may share his holiness." (Hebrews 12:10). "As he who called you is holy, be holy yourselves in every aspect of your conduct, for it is written, 'Be holy because I [am] holy.'" (1 Peter 1:15-16).

Divinization is, above all, a call to become part of the family of God. We are gifted with Jesus, the Son of God become man. We are called to live with his Life. In so doing we become his brothers and sisters. We become children of God in a new sense: we literally receive the Life of God and can call God our Father in the fullest sense. As has often been said, the parable of the Prodigal Son may be better described as the Parable of the Prodigal Father. It is the Father who gives "prodigally," whose love knows no bounds.

We who squander our "inheritance on a life of dissipation" (Luke 15:13) are brought to our "senses" (15:17) to "get up and go to my father" (15:18) by the Holy Spirit. "For those who are led by the Spirit of God are children of God. For you did not receive a spirit of slavery to fall back into fear, but you received a spirit of adoption, through which we cry, "Abba, Father!" The Spirit itself bears witness with our spirit that we are children of God." (Romans 8: 14-16). As we begin our journey home it is the Father who comes to receive us: "While he was still a long way off, his father caught sight of him, and was filled with compassion. He ran to his son, embraced him and kissed him." (Luke 15:20).

In his joy, he cries out, "Then let us celebrate with a feast, because this son of mine was dead, and has come to life again; he was lost, and has been found.' Then the celebration began." (Luke 20:23-4). The feast laid out before us by the Holy Spirit is the Eucharist. The Father's Gift to us who have squandered all that we have received is his only-begotten Son.

Appendix 1

The Scientific Quest for the Origin of Life – a Status Report from Researchers

Simon Conway Morris, Professor of Palaeobiology, Cambridge Univerity: "Amongst the many oddities of life is that fact that first there is no detailed instruction manual - and in this context we can effectively ignore the genetic code - but these systems, if prodded or disrupted, are remarkably adept at self-repair. ... So too however neglected it may be because of its sheer familiarity, too easily we forget the remarkable homeostasis of living organisms, that is their internal balance and capacity for adjustment whatever the external environment. ... Not only is the integrity and integration of living systems quite astonishing, but attempts to employ machine-like analogies soon run into difficulties. ... The reality is that organisms have a subtlety and efficiency far beyond any machine we can build. Again and again we discover that even in apparently straightforward functions there is an exactness to purpose which is eerily precise. The fact remains we have no idea of what it is about life that although obviously made of atoms no different then you find in a stone combines to form such a dynamic entity, culminating in the entirely surprising ability to become conscious. ... The sum of the parts that defines life will continue to elude us if we insist on constructing definitions that look no further than a physico-chemical basis."[1]

Carl Woese, the world's leading microbiologist: "In some sense, the genetic code is a fossil or perhaps an echo of the origin of life, just as the cosmic microwave background is a sort of echo of the Big Bang. And its form points to a process very different from today's Darwinian evolution.' Woese argues that nothing in the modern synthesis explains how evolution could have produced the genetic code and the basic genetic machinery used by all organisms, especially the enzymes and structures involved in translating genetic information into proteins."[2]

Jeffrey L. Bada and Antonio Lazcano, two of the world's leading origin-of-life researchers:

> "It is not possible to assign a precise chronology to the appearance of life."

> "How the ubiquitous genetic system of extant life based on nucleic acid originated is one of the major unsolved problems in contemporary biology."

> "Although there have been considerable advances in the understanding of chemical processes that may have taken place before the emergence of the first living entities, life's beginnings are still shrouded in mystery."[3]

Gustavo Caetano-Anollés: "The "RNA world" hypothesis, first promoted in 1986 in a paper in the journal Nature and defended and elaborated on for more than 25 years, posits that the first stages of molecular evolution involved RNA and not proteins, and that proteins (and DNA) emerged later, said University of Illinois crop sciences and Institute for Genomic Biology professor Gustavo Caetano-Anollés, who led the new study. 'I'm convinced that the RNA world (hypothesis) is not correct,' Caetano-Anollés said. 'That world of nucleic acids could not have existed if not tethered to proteins.' … 'This is the crucial piece of the puzzle,' Caetano-Anollés said. 'If the evolutionary build-up of ribosomal proteins and RNA and the interactions between them occurred gradually, step-by-step, the origin of the ribosome cannot be the product of an RNA world. Instead, it must be the product of a ribonucleoprotein world, an ancient world that resembles our own. It appears the basic building blocks of the machinery of the cell have always been the same from the beginning of life to the present: evolving and interacting proteins and RNA molecules.'"[4]

John Horgan, *Scientific American*:
[Craig] Venter's team synthesized and modified DNA from one type of bacteria and inserted the artificial genome into another bacterial species whose own DNA had been extracted. "The form of life that was created was not new," Mark Bedau, a philosopher at Reed College and editor of the journal *Artificial Life*, said in *Science*. "What was essentially done was the *re-creation* of an existing bacterial form of life, except that it was given a prosthetic genome (synthesized in the laboratory), and except that the genome was put into the cytoplasm of a slightly different species."

As Bedau and others point out, scientists still have not come close to creating a living organism from nonbiological materials, especially ones that might have existed on Earth four billion years ago. In other words, scientists have not shown how life began, how inanimate materials become animate.

This problem of life's origin appears harder today than in 1953, after a 23-year-old graduate student named Stanley Miller filled a glass chamber with methane, ammonia, hydrogen (representing the atmosphere) and water (the oceans). A spark- discharge device zapped the gases with simulated lightning while a heating coil kept the waters bubbling. Within a few days the water and gases were stained with a reddish goo rich in amino acids, the building blocks of proteins. (Jeffrey Bada, a biochemist and former student of Miller, recently reanalyzed Miller's old samples and discovered that they contain even more amino acids than Miller had realized.)

Miller and other scientists thought that they would quickly demonstrate in detail how genesis unfolded, but that hasn't happened. When I interviewed Miller in the early 1990s, he admitted that the problem of life's origin had turned out to be much harder than he had imagined. He was nonetheless still confident that one day scientists would crack the riddle of life's origin: "It will be in the nature of something that will make you say, 'There it is. How could you have overlooked this for so long?' And everybody will be totally convinced." Miller died three years ago, his dream unfulfilled.

There are now almost as many theories of life's origin as there are theorists. Perhaps the most popular is the "RNA world" theory, which posits ribonucleic acid as the first biomolecule. Whereas DNA cannot replicate without the help of enzymes, RNA can act as it own enzyme, snipping itself in two and splicing itself back together again. But RNA and its components are difficult to synthesize in a laboratory, let alone under plausible prebiotic conditions. Moreover, once RNA is synthesized it can make new copies of itself only with a great deal of coaxing by a chemist. Stanley Miller, among others, believed that some simpler—and possibly quite dissimilar— molecule must have paved the way for RNA, but no strong candidate has emerged.

Arthur Caplan declares that Venter and other scientists have dispelled the notion that life "is sacred, special, ineffable and beyond human understanding." Wrong. We still have no idea how life began, or whether life exists only here on our lonely planet or pervades the cosmos. One of the great ironies of modern science is that as we gain more power over life, it remains as fundamentally mysterious as ever.[5]

A report from the Carnegie Institution for Science conference on the origin of life observes that "despite significant progress on both ends, a vast gulf persists separating our understanding of the geochemistry of early Earth, and the biomolecules it could produce, from what we know of the most ancient life."[6]

There is strong disagreement on the site where life originated. As *Scientific American* reports, "Synthetic chemists generally favour a continental origin and geologists and biologist mostly deep-sea hydrothermal vents. Chemists argue it's impossible to do the chemistry in hydrothermal vents, while biologists argue that the terrestrial chemistry proposed just isn't like anything seen in biochemistry and doesn't narrow the gap between geochemistry and biochemistry."[7]

What is clear today is that life appeared in a relatively short period after the earth had cooled down.

ENDNOTES

Chapter 1

[1] St. Athanasius, *Letters to Serapion*, 1,24.
[2] St. Cyril of Jerusalem, *Dialogue* VII.
[3] *Philokalia, Volume II*, translated and edited by G.E.H. Palmer, Philip Sherrard, and Kallistos Ware (London: Faber and Faber, 1982), 240.
[4] St. Ambrose, *On the Mysteries*, (Nn. 52-54. 58: SC 25 bis, 186-188. 190).
[5] St. Basil the Great, *On the Holy Spirit*, 27.

Chapter 2

[1] Arvindaksha Menon, op cit., 90ff.
[2] Krishna Mohan Banerjea, *The Arian Witness* (Calcutta: Thacker, Spink & Co., 1875), 200, 206, 210
[3] http://www.hindu.com/thehindu/thscrip/print.pl?file=2007040701390100.htm&date=2007/04/07/&prd=mp&
[4] Geoffrey Parrinder, *World Religions – From Ancient History to the Present* (New York: Facts on File, 1983), 181.
[5] Cited in Timothy Freke and Peter Gandy, *The Jesus Mysteries* (London: Thorsons, 1999), 327.
[6] *History of Zoroastrianism* (New York: Ams Pr Inc, 1938), 254.
[7] Chan Kei Thong, *Faith of Our Fathers – God in Ancient China* (Shanghai, China: Orient Publishing Group, 2006), 164.
[8] Ibid., 157-8.
[9] Walter Burkert, *Homo Necans: The Anthropology of Ancient Greek Sacrificial Ritual and Myth*, transl. Peter Bing (Berkeley, California: University of California Press, 1983), 9-10

¹⁰Henry Clay Trumbull, *The Blood Covenant* (Kirkwood, MO: Impact Books, 1975), 202.

Chapter 3

¹Martin K. Barrack, *Second Exodus* (Houston: Magnificat Institute Press, 1999), 179.
²Brant Pitre, *Jesus and the Jewish Roots of the Eucharist* (New York: Doubleday, 2011), 90.
³Ibid., 121.
⁴Ibid.,125, 128-130, 132-3.

Chapter 5

¹St. Athanasius, *De incarnatione*, 54, 3: PG 25, 192B.
²St. Ephraem of Syria, *Hymns on Faith* 5.17 (Corpus Scriptorum Christianorum Orientalium 155.17).
³Maximus the Confessor, *Selected Writings*, tr. George Berthold (Mahwah, NJ: Paulist Press, 1985), 83-4.
⁴Council of Ephesus (431).
⁵http://www.columbia.edu/cu/augustine/a/cucharist-q.html.
⁶Robert Sungenis, *Not By Bread Alone: The Biblical and Historical Evidence for the Eucharistic Sacrifice* (Goleta, CA: Queenship Publishing, 2000), 163.
⁷*The Gospel of John*, trans., G.R. Beasley-Murray (Philadelphia, PA: Westminster Press, 1971), 236.
⁸Robert Sungenis, op cit., 169 ff.
⁹"On Transubstantiation," pamphlet, London, 1974, 111.
¹⁰Joachim Jeremias, *The Eucharistic Words of Jesus*, translated by Norman Perrin, (Philadelphia: Fortress Press, 1966), 170-71.
¹¹Otto Betz, *Das Mahl de herrn bei Paulus* (Tubingen: Mohr Siebeck, 1990), 217-51.
¹²Stanley Jaki, *Why the Mass?* (Pinckney, Michigan: Real View Books, 2003). 13-4.
¹³Ibid., 28.
¹⁴Robert Sungenis, op cit., 133.
¹⁵E.L. Mascall, *Corpus Christi* (London: Longmans, 1965), 189. 16Brant Pitre, *Jesus, the Tribulation and the End of the Exile* (Grand Rapids, Michigan: Baker Academic, 2005), 443

[17] Brant Pitre, *Jesus and the Jewish Roots of the Eucharist*, op cit., 169.
[18] Pinchas Lapide, *The Resurrection of Jesus – A Jewish Perspective* (Minneapolis: Augsburg Publishing House), 1983, 125-6. 19Ludwig Wittgenstein, *Culture and Value*, transl. Peter Winch (Oxford: Blackwell, 1980),33.
[20] Stanley Jaki, *Why Believe in Jesus* (Pinckney, Michigan: Real View Books, 2002), 46-9.
[21] http://worshipspot.blogspot.com/2005/04/sacrifice-by-renowned-hindu-scholar.html.
[22] Chan Kei Thong, *Faith of Our Fathers – God in Ancient China* (Shanghai: Orient Publishing Center, 2006), 317-9.
[23] Stanley Jaki, *Why Believe in Jesus* (Pinckney, Michigan: Real View Books, 2002), 39-40.
[24] Eugenio Zolli, *The Nazarene* translated by Cyril Vollert (New Hope, Kentucky: Ut et Orbi and Remnant of Israel, 1999), 190-5.
[25] Stephen Pimentel, "The Eucharistic Tabernacle in the Book of Hebrews," paper.
[26] http://www.hindu.com/thehindu/thscrip/print.pl?file=2007040701390100.htm&date=2007/04/07/&prd=mp&
[27] John Breck, *Spirit of Truth* (Yonkers, New York: St. Vladimir's Seminary Press, 1991).
[28] Roger Beck, *Beck on Mithraism* (Aldersgate: Aldershot, Hampshire, Great Britain, 2004), 118.
[29] Rene Girard, *Violence and the Sacred* (NY: Continuum, 1988), 264.
[30] Wendy Doniger O'Flaherty, *Other Peoples' Myths* (University of Chicago Press, 1995), 106-107.
[31] Jonathan Z. Smith, "Dying and Rising Gods" in *Encyclopedia of Religion ed.* Mircea Eliade (New York: Macmillan, 1987), Volume 4, 521.
[32] Hugo Rahner, *Greek Myths and Christian Mystery* (London: Burns and Oates, 1963), 31.
[33] Ibid., 34.
[34] Ibid., 34-5.
[35] Charles Hoffman, *Twice Chosen* (Goleta, CA: Queenship, 1995), 51.
36Brant Pitre,*Jesus and the Jewish Roots of the Eucharist*, op cit., 98, 102-3, 189.
[37] Ibid., 95.
[38] *The Lamb's Supper* (New York: Doubleday, 1999), 119.
[39] Scott Hahn, *Swear to God* (New York: Doubleday, 2004), 142-5.

⁴⁰Eugenio Zolli, "The Influence of Hebrew Religion Upon Christian Liturgy", Lecture 10, July 3, 1953; Lecture 9, July 9, 1953; Lecture 13, July 8, 1953. (University of Notre Dame, Indiana, transcribed by Sister M. Gerard, S.C.M.M.).
⁴¹Roch Kereszty, "The Eucharist of the Church and the One Self-Offering of Christ" in *Rediscovering the Eucharist* edited by Roch Kereszty (Mahwah, New Jersey: Paulist Press, 2003), 244.
⁴²Robert Sungenis, op cit., 177.
⁴³Henry Clay Trumbull, op cit., 274-5, 281-2.
⁴⁴Brant Pitre, *Jesus and the Jewish Roots of th72t*, op cit., 75.
⁴⁵Ibid., 76.
⁴⁶Ibid., 115.
⁴⁷Bruce Metzger, *Historical and Literary Studies: Pagan, Jewish, and Christian* (Grand Rapids: Eerdmans, 1968), 11.
⁴⁸Robert Sokolowski, *Eucharistic Presence* (Washington D.C.: Catholic University of America Press, 1994), 228-9.
⁴⁹Dan Merkur, *Gnosis* (1993, State University of New York Press, Albany), 129.
⁵⁰Stephen Clark, *Catholics and the Eucharist* (Ann Arbor, Michigan: Servant Publications, 2000), 150.

Chapter 6

¹St. Athanasius, *De incarnatione*, 54, 3: PG 25, 192B.
²*Adversus Haereses*, Book 5, Preface.
³Stromata Book 1:8.
⁴*Oration* 30:14. *A Select Library of Nicene and Post-Nicene Fathers of the Christian Church*, second series, 14 vols. (Grand Rapids, MI: Eerdmans, 1989), 7:315.
⁵*In Ioannem*, 9.
⁶St. Gregory of Nazianzus quoting St. Basil in "Funeral Oration for St. Basil" in Stavropoulus, *Nature*, 18.
⁷*The Great Catechism*, ch. 37 in *Gregory of Nyssa*, Vol. 5 of *NPNF*, ed. Philip Schaff (Garland, TX: Galaxy Software, 2000) CD-ROM.)
⁸St. Augustine's Expositions on the Book of Psalms: Nicene and Post-Nicene Fathers of the Christian Church, Volume 8, edited by Schaff, Philip (New York: Christian Literature Publishing Co., 1886), 178

[9] "Various Texts on Theology, the Divine Economy, and Virtue and Vice", *The Philokalia, The Complete Text*, 5 vols. trans. G. E. H. Palmer et. al, (Boston: Faber, 1981), 2:181.
[10] *Ennarationes in Psalmos*, 49.1.2.
[11] Timothy Ware, *The Orthodox Church* (New York: Pelican, 1993), 236.
[12] St. Athanasius, Ep Serap. 1, 24:PG 26, 585 and 588.
[13] St. Cyril of Jerusalem (Dialogue VII).
[14] St. Basil, *On the Holy Spirit*, ch. 1 quoted in Daniel B. Clendenin, *Partakers of Divinity: The Orthodox Doctrine of Theosis*, 371.
[15] *Ad Max* 2; Letter 61.2.
[16] Maximus the Confessor, *Selected Writings*, (Mahwah, NJ: Paulist Press, 1985), tr. George Berthold, 83-4.
[17] Michael L. Gaudoin-Parker ed. *The Real Presence Through the Ages* (New York: Alba House, 1993), 8.
[18] Chapter 9.
[19] Chapter 66.
[20] *The Epistle of Ignatius to the Smyraeans*, Chapter VIII.
[21] Cited in James T. O'Connor, *The Hidden Manna* (San Francisco: Ignatius Press, 1988), 15.
[22] Michael L. Gaudoin-Parker ed. *The Real Presence Through the Ages*, op cit., 19.
[23] Ibid., 33.
[24] Ibid., 35.
[25] Excerpts from: Sermon 227.
[26] Stanley Jaki, *Why the Mass?* (Pinckney, Michigan: Real View Books, 2003). 25.
[27] J.N.D. Kelly, *Early Christian Doctrines* (San Francisco, CA: Harper and Row, 1978), 214.
[28] Robert Sungenis, *Not By Bread Alone: The Biblical and Historical Evidence for the Eucharistic Sacrifice* (Goleta, CA: Queenship Publishing, 2000), 112.
[29] M.J. Scheeben, *The Mysteries of Christianity* (St. Louis: Herder, 1950), 509.
[30] *Homilies on Hebrews* 11, 2-3; *On the Priesthood* 3,4.
[31] *Corpus Christi*, (London: Longmans, 1965), 132-5.
[32] Scott Hahn, *The Lamb's Supper* (New York: Doubleday, 1999), 150-1.

Chapter 7

[1] Marc Hauser, "The Origin of the Mind," *Scientific American* September 2009, 44-51.
[2] J. Andrew Ross, "First-Person Consciousness," *Journal of Consciousness Studies*, 9, No. 7, 2002, 260.
[3] George Wald, "Life and Mind in the Universe," in Henry Margenau and Roy Abraham Varghese ed. *Cosmos, Bios, Theos* (La Salle: Open Court, 1992), 218.
[4] Sir John Eccles, "A Divine Design: Some Questions on Origins," in Henry Margenau and Roy Abraham Varghese ed. *Cosmos, Bios, Theos* (La Salle: Open Court, 1992), 164.
[5] Gerald Schroeder, *The Hidden Face of God* (New York: The Free Press, 2001).
[6] William P. Alston, "Substance and the Trinity," in *The Trinity* edited by Stephen T. Davis and Gerald O'Collins, (Oxford: Oxford University Press, 1999).) David Odenberg is today's leading contemporary defender of the coherence of the concept of substance.
[7] Josef Seifert, *What is Life?* (Amsterdam-Atlanta, GA: Rodopi, 1997), 59, 60.
[8] http://www.usccb.org/dpp/realpresencc.htm. 9 *Summa Theologica*, 3-76-1.
[10] *Summa*, 3-75-3-Reply to Objection 1.
[11] *Summa*, 3-77-5.
[12] *Summa*, 3-75-6- Reply to Objection 2.
[13] *142nd* Homily on Luke http://blogs.nd.edu/oblation/2011/08/17/the-drug-of-immortality- eucharistic-liturgy-and-eschatology-part-vii/
[14] *Commentary on the Gospel of John* (Lib. 4, 2: PG 73, 563-566).
[15] *Summa*, 3-76-3-3.
[16] *Summa*, 3-75-1-3.
[17] *Summa*, 3-76-6.
[18] St. John Chyrsostom, *pro. Jud.* 1:5: J. P. Migne, ed., *Patrologia Graeca* (Paris, 1857-1866) 49, 380.
[19] St. Ambrose, *De myst.* 9, 50; 52: J. P. Migne, ed., Patrologia Latina (Paris: 1841-1855) 16, 405-407.
[20] Albert Einstein in *The World Treasury of Physics, Astronomy and Mathematics* edited by Timothy Ferris (Boston: Little, Brown and Company, 1991), 58.

Chapter 8

[1] *Summa Theologica,* 3-77-6.

Appendix

[1] "Darwin's Compass" (http://www.faith.org.uk/publications/Magazines/Nov05/Nov05Darwi nsCompass.html) [1]
[2] "Horizontal and vertical: The evolution of evolution," Mark Buchanan, New Scientist 26 January 2010. http://www.newscientist.com/article/mg20527441.500-horizontal-and-vertical-the-evolution-of-evolution.html?full=true&print=true [2]
[3] *The Origin of Life,* 7/11/2008, 72.
[4] "Early Evolution of Life: Study of Ribosome Evolution Challenges 'RNA World' Hypothesis", *ScienceDaily (Mar. 12, 2012).*
[5] http://www.scientificamerican.com/blog/post.cfm?id=craig-venter-has-neither-creatednor-2010-05-27
[6] https://doi.org/10.1098/rsta.2016.0337
[7] https://www.scientificamerican.com/article/lifes-origins-by-land-or-sea-debate-gets-hot/

www.ingramcontent.com/pod-product-compliance
Lightning Source LLC
Chambersburg PA
CBHW051547010526
44118CB00022B/2610